ARGENTINE CINEMA

Eugenio Py, director of Argentina's first film, La bandera argentina *(The Argentine Flag, 1897), seen here filming naval exercises at the turn of the century.*

ARGENTINE CINEMA
edited by Tim Barnard

Nightwood Editions   Toronto

Acknowledgements

FERNANDO BIRRI, "The Roots of Documentary Realism," translated by Julianne Burton, reprinted from *Cinema and Social Change in Latin America: Conversations with Filmmakers*, University of Texas Press, Austin, 1986. "For a Nationalist, Realist, Critical and Popular Cinema," translated by Michael Chanan, reprinted from *Screen*, Volume 26, no. 3-4, May-August 1985.
JORGE LUIS BORGES, film reviews, translated by Ronald Christ and Gloria Waldman, reprinted from *Borges in/and/on Film*, by Edgardo Cozarinsky, Lumen, New York, 1986.
JULIO CORTAZAR, "Lucas, His Friends," translated by Gregory Rabassa, reprinted from *A Certain Lucas*, Alfred A. Knopf, New York, 1984.
EDGARDO COZARINSKY, "Partial Enchantments of Narrative," translated by Ronald Christ and Gloria Waldman, reprinted from *Borges in/and/on Film*, Lumen, New York, 1986.
OCTAVIO GETINO, "Some Notes on the Concept of a 'Third Cinema'," reprinted from *Notas sobre cine argentino y latinamericano*, Edimedios, Mexico, 1984.
ALFONSO GUMUCIO DAGRON, "Argentina: A Huge Case of Censorship," reprinted from *Cine, censura y exilio en América Latina*, STUNAM-CIMCA-FEM, Mexico, 1984.

Cover design by Maureen Cochrane. Typeset, produced, and published by Nightwood Editions, Box 5432, Station A, Toronto, Ontario M5W 1N6 Canada (416-534-0392) / A division of blewointmentpress ltd.

Published with the assistance of the block grant programs of the Canada Council and the Ontario Arts Council. Printed in Canada.

ISBN 0-88971-106-2

The publication of *Argentine Cinema* was made possible by the generous cooperation of the Ontario Film Institute.

Table of Contents

*Dedicated to the memory of Ed, a printer by trade,
and to Douglas and Eleanor.*

Note re. translations

Many of the films discussed in this book do not appear in any of the existing English-language literature on Argentine cinema. Those films with very idiomatic titles that the editor has not been able to view have thus remained untranslated. Future scholars may want to revise those translations that are provided; perhaps with time standard English titles might be arrived at.

Photo acknowledgements

The photographs in this volume appear through the kind permission of the following publishers and organizations:

Calistro, Mariano, et al., eds., *Reportaje al cine argentino: los pioneros del sonoro*, Anesa, Buenos Aires, 1978, front cover & pp. 24, 28-30, 34, 37, 44, 48.

Cine Libre, Volume 1, No. 3/4, Buenos Aires, 1983, p. 144.

Couselo, Jorge Miguel, ed., *Historia del cine argentino*, Centro Editor de América Latina, Buenos Aires, 1984, back cover, frontispiece & pp. 22, 26, 42, 52, 55, 78.

España, Claudio, ed., *Medio siglo de cine: Argentina Sono Film*, Editorial Abril/Heraldo del Cine, Buenos Aires, 1984, pp. 33, 40.

Gumucio Dagron, Alfonso, *Cine, censura y exilio en América Latina*, STUNAM/CIMCA/FEM, Mexico, 1984 (2nd edition), p. 98.

Museo del Cine Pablo C. Ducrós Hicken, Buenos Aires, pp. 6, 9, 13, 15, 17, 19, 20, 21, 23, 31, 46, 50, 53, 54, 56, 63.

Foreword

This monograph on Argentine cinema has been prepared with a view to providing a general introduction to the subject in light of the renewed interest in Argentine cinema which has followed the end of military rule in 1983. At the same time, it is hoped that the issues discussed in the articles reprinted here might serve as signposts for future scholars preparing more thorough commentaries on Argentine cinema. The scarcity of translations of critical documents coming out of current debates within national cinemas is startling, particularly in English. Of the major articles included here, for example, only one has previously appeared in English, and none have appeared in book form (although two of the articles are excerpted from interesting forthcoming publications, as indicated in the acknowledgements). It is essential that texts such as these begin to appear abroad in translation with greater regularity, and not just in specialized journals.

No attempt has been made to maintain a thematic unity between the articles reproduced here; such a task would have been impossible in any event. The reader may thus perceive some of the fundamental disparities in critical analysis that have historically marked Argentine cultural and intellectual life. In the context of the polarization of the country's social classes and its neo-colonial status, these different critical perspectives have come to be seen as exclusive and incompatible.

It has been impossible as well to include discussions of some of the most vital sectors of the national film industry. This lack should be redressed by future scholars. Limitations of time and space have precluded reprinting appreciations of the important *nuevo cine* movement of the 1950s and '60s, as well as of the strong tradition of ethnographic filmmaking, particularly visible in the work of Jorge Prelorán and now undergoing a renewal in newly democratic Argentina. A more substantial absence, and one not so easily solved, is that of women contributors and discussions of the place of women in the national film industry. This absence is a reflection of the continued exclusion of women from the feature film industry — at present, only one woman, María Luisa Bemberg, makes features with any regularity — and from intellectual life in general. There are presently several female cultural comment-ators at work in the country, and it is hoped that they soon turn their attention to the cinema, as it should be hoped that the talented women in the national film school persevere and contribute regularly to national production.

This publication was prepared to accompany a retrospective of Argentine cinema at the Ontario Film Institute in Toronto and at film institutes across Canada in early 1987. This program has been prepared by Jacqueline Kuehnel and myself for the OFI. I would like to take this opportunity to thank the many people who have lent their time and expertise in helping us to prepare this book and the film retrospective.

Manuel Antín and his staff at the *Instituto Nacional de Cinematografía* and Guillermo Fernández Jurado and his staff at the *Museo del Cine Pablo C. Ducrós Hicken* in Buenos Aires extended Ms Kuehnel and myself the warmest hospitality and provided invaluable assistance during our recent visit there.

Fernando Birri, Julianne Burton, Michael Chanan, Ronald Christ, Edgardo Cozarinsky, Octavio Getino, Alfonso Gumucio Dagron, Gloria Waldman, and the *Sindicato de la Industria Cinematográfica Argentina (SICA)* have graciously permitted us to reprint their work.

Al Cedrez, Alfredo Marchevsky, Beatriz Munárriz and Alex Zisman prepared those translations that were done exclusively for this volume. Ms Munárriz also helped in the translation of film titles throughout the book, and all provided their services for free, due to the unfortunate and excessively nationalistic regulations of Canadian arts funding bodies, which make work of this sort ineligible for grant monies.

Marc Glassman and Rose Marie and Roy Wolfe read an early

draft of my Chronology of Argentine Cinema, appended to this volume, and made invaluable comments on it. My introductory essay included here benefitted similarly from comments by Stephen Dale. Neither article would have been presentable without their advice, and any stylistic gaffes that remain surely do so over their protests.

While in Buenos Aires, further assistance was given Ms Kuehnel and myself by our friends Rafael Filippelli, Annemarie Heinrich, Teo Kofman, María Angeles Mira, Gustavo Mosquera R., José Nun, Alicia Sanguinetti, Fernando Solanas, Gerardo Vallejo, and Jorge Ventura and the staff of *SICA*.

Julianne Burton, Alberto Ciria, Marc Glassman, Wendy Rolph and Ambassador Francisco José Pullit and Eduardo Jantus at the Argentine Embassy provided further assistance and support in Canada and the U.S.

My own contributions to this volume were prepared with the assistance of the Ontario Arts Council, which made sure the rent was paid these past few months.

For my understanding of Argentine cinema and society I am indebted to Rafael Filippelli, Octavio Getino, Teo Kofman, Jacqueline Kuehnel, Alfredo Marchevsky, María Angeles Mira, Gustavo Mosquera R., Beatriz Munárriz, José Nun, Héctor Olivera, Osvaldo Pederoso, Alicia Sanguinetti, Fernando Solanas, Gerardo Vallejo, and, once again, to the many people at the *Instituto* and the *Museo*; all have patiently answered my questions and shared their unique insights with me.

Last, but certainly not least, my thanks to Gerald Pratley and Sherie Brethour at the Ontario Film Institute and Maureen Cochrane and David Lee at Nightwood Editions for their unstinting support, and to Jacqueline Kuehnel for her invaluable assistance.

Tim Barnard

Toronto
August 1986

Popular Cinema and Populist Politics
Tim Barnard

In preparing the material for this article, I have relied heavily on the work of the major historians of Argentine film. Most of the material on the pre-1960 period is taken from Domingo di Núbila's definitive two-volume history of Argentine cinema (1960). (Beware of the 16-page English "summary" of this work: evidently prepared under the military government sometime in the 1960s, and still circulating in film libraries around the world, it severely distorts Mr. di Núbila's original comments on the period of Perón's first presidencies, from 1946-55, as the military governments that succeeded Perón were intent on erasing his memory and discrediting his rule). Other major sources of information on Argentine cinema were the histories by Jorge Miguel Couselo, ed. (1984) and Octavio Getino (1978). My conversations with Mr. Getino two years ago may be said to have planted the seed for this article and my analysis owes much to him. The work of José Augustín Mahieu (1966 and 1974), though due to circumstance not consulted extensively here, is also a major contribution to the history of Argentine cinema.

As I have not been able to see many of the films discussed here, and because of space limitations, I have not considered the artistic merit of individual films in detail. In the case of films I have not seen, I have relied on the above historians' accounts of them in my analysis.

My discussion of U.S. foreign policy in Latin America during the critical 1942-55 period, and of the management of the Argentine film industry during that same period, is a synthesis of the research of Jorge Schnitman (1984), Gaizka Usabel (1982), and Mr. di Núbila. My brief survey of Argentine history in the 19th century, and much of my understanding of modern Argentine politics, benefitted from lectures on these topics by Professor José Nun at the University of Toronto and on my subsequent discussions with him.

These acknowledgements, because of the haste with which this article was prepared and the extent that I have borrowed from other peoples' work, must take the place of proper footnotes. However, since I have referred to many sources other than those mentioned above, and because all have been subjected to my own interpretation, I must accept responsibility for any errors or misinterpretations that remain.

Mario Soffici (centre) on the set of Prisioneros de la tierra

The influence of Argentine political life on the fortunes of the country's film industry, so forcefully felt during the period of the military dictatorship of 1976-83, has not always been the determinant factor in the industry's discontinuous, at times paroxysmic, development. Thus the year 1931 marks, paradoxically, the date of both the country's first military coup and of the birth of the national sound film industry, destined to become the continent's largest until its decline in the 1940s. The political repression of the 1930s, *la decada infame*, did not impede the growth of the film industry, as the dictatorship of 1976-83 did so brutally. Nor did it prevent the birth of Latin America's first socially critical film genre, the "social-folkloric," that peaked in the late 1930s and early 1940s with films such as Mario Soffici's *Prisioneros de la tierra* (Prisoners of the Earth, 1939). Soffici and others built a tentative but extremely popular social criticism genre in the mainstream film industry, rooted in popular national culture, in spite of a censorship that Soffici has said kept him from examining religious issues and treating his political topics in as much depth as he would have liked.* While the other genres that flourished in this era lack this element of social criticism they were, I will argue, fundamentally linked to Argentine popular culture and history in a way that had unmistakable political implications. In a country that has regularly seen pitched battles between the national bourgeoisie and the working classes for control of the culture industries, the film industry in this period was the almost exclusive domain of the latter, producing popular genres in a characteristically national style.

The period of the film industry's rapid artistic and economic decline in the mid 1940s is another example of the independent course the industry has taken from national political life. Colonel Juan Domingo Perón first appeared in Argentine politics as a participant in the military coup of 1943. He subsequently became Secretary of Labour and Social Welfare and introduced the first legislation governing the Argentine film industry. In 1946 he began a decade of rule as President of the Republic, introducing a period of fierce economic and cultural nationalism, a populist brand of politics, and remark-

* Quoted in Calistro et. al. (1978).

ably progressive labour and social welfare policies. This, then, was a period that might have been expected to nurture the growth and populist traditions of the national film industry. It was precisely during Perón's rule, however, for reasons I will discuss below, that the film industry abruptly turned its back on the popular form and national themes of the 1930s in favour of European sources and a bourgeois form. The result of this strategy was to alienate the industry's largest markets, the Argentine and Latin American working classes, and bring ruin to the industry. It should be clear, then, that the peculiar dynamics of the national film industry must be explained with reference to autonomous social and cultural forces as much as to the country's often calamitous political events of the past half-century.

It was not until 1973 that the film industry really took its cue from national political events: it was in that year that Perón returned to power from eighteen years of exile and the film industry collaborated in the political and social project that began to unfold in his name. For the first time since the early 1940s, the industry regained a synthesis of social criticism and a popular and distinctly Argentine style. Not coincidentally, it was in 1973 that production levels and attendance figures reached a level that had not been attained since that earlier era. In 1973, even the mainstream elements of the film industry had become politicized by the years of popular resistance that precipitated the military's downfall and Perón's return. It was in this context that Héctor Olivera's *La Patagonia rebelde* (Rebellion in Patagonia, 1974) was made. It was a strictly commercial endeavour by a mainstream director, and proved to be the most popular Argentine film during Perón's last presidency. The film is a gaucho epic of sorts, a traditional Argentine genre, but one laced with radical political rhetoric. As a depiction of the massacre of anarcho-syndicalist workers in Patagonia in the 1920s by a cold-blooded military, it was widely seen as an allegory for the bitter civil war that preceded Perón's return in 1973.* Today, as the country lives through a roughly analogous process — the return to democracy and

* See the entry regarding this film in the chronology of Argentine cinema, page 158, for an account of its impact on Argentine society.

8

the rebirth of national culture — the production strategies of the mainstream of the film industry are vastly different, and it seems as if the goal of synthesizing a popular national style with social criticism has been abandoned. The reasons for this must be sought, first of all, in the events of 1976-83, but also in the long-standing national cultural conflict which is a product of the extreme polarization of Argentina's social classes.

The most recent and extreme period of political repression in Argentina — begun in 1974 by the Peronist Right after the death of Perón and intensifed under the Junta of 1976-83 — is coming to be characterized as a period of abberational terror. Some political commentators of the non-Peronist Left, however, are insisting that the Junta's activities be seen instead as a culmination, even as a logical outgrowth, of Argentina's economic and political history.* This position shifts the focus of attention from newspaper-headline body-counts of atrocities to a consideration of what the Junta's long-term objectives were; whether, in fact, they were not at least

* See especially Dabat and Lorenzano (1984).

La Patagonia rebelde *(Rebellion in Patagonia)*

partially achieved; and to what extent they continue to inform the political and social agendas of the highest levels of the national bourgeoisie.

Similar questions come to mind about the Junta's cultural policies (and it must be remembered that the Junta had a planned and ambitious cultural, economic, and political agenda. Theirs was neither a policy of containment nor of "blind terror" but a plan to restructure Argentine society on a scale without parallel in our hemisphere in this century). Beyond the assassinations, the exiles, and the blacklists, what were the effects of the Junta's policies on the Argentine film industry? What was the long-term cultural agenda of the Junta and how might it be seen as a culmination of long-standing conflicts in Argentine cultural history?

It is fairly simple to catalogue some of the structural effects of the Junta's rule on the film industry. Production fell to its lowest level in twenty years, since the period following Perón's overthrow in 1955. The industry was subsequently affected by massive unemployment and union activities were suspended. Foreign markets were lost — a disaster in an industry that has always relied on international sales for its survival. There were huge drops in domestic movie attendance and widespread movie theatre closings, particular in the interior of the country. The domestic market became dominated as never before by U.S. films — second-rate ones at that, as better productions were stopped at the border because of everything from nudity to references to homosexuality and other forms of "immorality." Production became concentrated in the hands of a few large firms — since 1977, there has been only one sound studio in the country. A distribution sector specializing in cheap U.S. imports was consolidated, as it became more advantageous to distribute foreign films and benefit from the lower capital investment they required and the greater rates of return they offered. Finally, a system of censorship was imposed that was not only so severe that meaningful social criticism became impossible, but so erratic and unpredictable that investment in national film production became a very risky proposition, as censored films would neither earn revenue in the domestic market nor be likely to be sold abroad. A censored film's producer would also be denied payment of promised state co-production assistance, which led to the ruin of at least one production company. Without going over each of these points in detail, it should be clear that such structural changes in the film industry must certainly be affecting current efforts to revive production, recover foreign markets, and re-establish a healthy domestic market.

Predictably, a decade of repression, an emasculated national production at drastically reduced levels, and a flood of generally poor foreign films led to a profound debasement of popular taste. Yet it is important to situate this process not just as a result of the policies and repression of the Junta but to relate it to a long-standing conflict in the national culture. Through its actions the Junta was simply enacting the agenda of one side in this conflict, albeit on an unprecedented scale. It should be noted that the Junta developed as apocalyptic a vision of national culture as it did of the country's political life. While the Junta believed that the entire Argentine political process had become tainted with the influences of "International Marxism," it remained for them a largely foreign threat, with Argentine agents.

Their analysis of popular culture was substantially different. Here, the danger lay within the unique political heritage of the country's popular culture, a heritage that had been revived and so forcefully expressed under Perón in the 1973-75 period. It thus became imperative to the Junta that they eliminate popular national culture in its entirety in order to "reconstruct" it. Culturally, perhaps even more so than politically, they had to shear off the cancer affecting Argentine society and start from zero, or lose the game. In this sense, the censorship, economic chaos, and genocide of the Junta's rule were just the growing pains of a project of "National Reconstruction" whose agenda was only beginning to be fulfilled.

Argentina's Social and Economic Development: 1810-1914

It would be beyond the scope of this article to undertake a proper overview of either Argentina's economic and social development or of the political traditions within its popular culture. I will instead map out a very cursory and much simplified survey of the salient points of Argentine history and economic development from independence to 1914. The latter date marks both the approximate end, with the beginning of the First War in Europe, of this formative period, as well as the birth of the national silent feature film. My concern throughout will be to relate this discussion to the dynamics of the later development of a national film culture. The history of the *gaucho*, for example, would later inspire the creation of a *gaucho* film genre, one which unmistakably represents the class and cultural conflicts that precipitated the military campaign against the *gauchos* in the last century.

In the early nineteenth century Argentina emerged from its colonial period dissimilar in many ways from its neighbours in the southern cone of the continent. In Brazil, the Portugese had imposed a ruinous plantation economy worked by slave labour. The Andean regions of present-day Peru, Bolivia and Chile were stripped of their mineral wealth by the Spaniards, who decimated the region's indigenous populations. Argentina's role in the colonial economy, in contrast, was minimal and late-starting. By the end of the eighteenth century the country was critically under-populated and neglected by Spain. Its indigenous populations had survived the conquest unmolested and, with the *mestizo* and white *gauchos*, lived off herds of wild cattle on the vast *pampa*, perhaps the world's richest agricultural lands. However, the Spaniards in Latin America were less interested in agriculture than in the importance of Buenos Aires as a seaport for shipping the continent's mineral wealth to Europe.

Inevitably, however, the merchant class of Buenos Aires set their sights on the *pampa* soon after independence was declared in 1810. Already, this class had become strongly influenced by European cultural and intellectual life and it shared the Positivistic ideas then in vogue in Europe. The port bourgeoisie sought to modernize Argentina, develop the *pampa*, and open the country up to the capital and culture of Europe.

However, a period of political instability and territorial fragmentation followed independence, lasting until late in the century. It was not until 1880 that Argentina could be said to be fully consolidated as a nation-state, after the establishment of a national currency, a single Armed Forces, a national legal code and — of critical importance to the Buenos Aires merchants — after the abolition of internal customs tariffs.

During much of this early post-independence period (1835-52), the country was ruled by the *caudillo* strongman Juan Manuel de Rosas. A landowner from the interior, Rosas was the political and cultural antithesis of the Buenos Aires bourgeoisie. His fervent nationalism, belief in a federal state structure as opposed to a unified republican one, and distrust of foreign capital prevented the country's modernization. It was not until his overthrow in 1852, long strived for by the national bourgeoisie, that the development of the *pampa* and the opening up of the country to foreign capital could begin. A military campaign led by General Roca in the 1870s exterminated the indigenous population and routed or killed the *gauchos*. By 1880, when Roca became President, the *pampa* was empty, and the country entered into a half-century of intensive economic development fueled by astronomical levels of foreign investment.

It is essential at this point to take note of the cultural dimension of this political drive to "irrigate the *pampa* with the blood of the *gauchos*." By the time Rosas took power

La guerra gaucha *(The Gaucho War), by Lucas Demare, 1942*

in 1835, the national bourgeoisie was already culturally alienated from Latin America and under the spell of Europe. While Rosas blocked the bourgeoisie's attempts to modernize the country, this polarization between the national culture of the interior, that of the *gauchos* and the land-owning *caudillos*, and the European culture of the port bourgeoisie grew. Three years before Rosas' downfall in 1852, one of the most important books in Argentine history appeared, one that addressed this conflict directly. Written by Domingo Faustino Sarmiento, a leading Positivist of the day who envisioned bringing such European reforms as public education to the country, it decried the backwardness of the interior and the brutal nationalism of Rosas. Its title, *Facundo: civilización y barbarie* (Facundo: Civilization and Barbarism) set out the terms of this conflict clearly: the rational, "civilized" culture of Europe should be transplanted to Argentina to do away with the "barbarism" of the interior, represented by the book's anti-hero, the *caudillo* Facundo. In his preface, Sarmiento declared that the ruthless Facundo "still lives! He will return! He lives in popular traditions, in politics, and in Rosas, his heir," and asked if Rosas, rather than being an aberration, didn't represent "a social manifestation, an expression of the way of life of a people?" This book, and the campaign against national elements it championed, foreshadowed the social antagonisms of modern Argentina and the resulting terror of 1976-83. Sarmiento railed against the brutal dictatorship of Rosas, and envisioned a liberal European culture in Argentina. His successors have long since abandoned such ideals in their campaigns against contemporary nationalist elements. It is in this context that we must situate, for example, the persistence — until recently — of the *gaucho* theme in Argentine popular cinema. Roughly analagous to the Western in form, the *gaucho* film carries with it a far different ideological meaning, due to the historical circumstances of the last century. The *gaucho*, unlike the cowboy of the Western, does not represent the vanguard of the civilizing colonial forces but rather the last barrier to colonialization. He evokes not the glory of the birth of a new culture — one shared, at least ideologically, by the audience — but the destruction of national culture at the hands of the national and foreign bourgeoisie, a theme seen most explicitly in films such as *La Patagonia rebelde* and *Juan*

Moreira (Leonardo Favio, 1975), both made during Perón's last presidency.

By 1880, then, Argentina had been consolidated and the *pampa* was ready to be developed. There remained two obstacles to this task: the lack of capital and technology and the country's underpopulation (there were only about two million people in Argentina in 1880). The former would be supplied by the British, who had long been interested in gaining a foothold in the country, first militarily and then commercially. At the beginning of the century, Britain had invaded and occupied Buenos Aires, and were driven off by its residents, who soon afterwards declared their independence from Spain. The British also invaded the Malvinas Islands in 1833 and have occupied them since. During Rosa's reign they strived to extend their commercial interests in the country as much as possible. Under the government of 1880, however, they received an invitation to come into the project of national modernization as full partners.

The new landed oligarchy in Argentina, members of the Buenos Aires merchant class who had parceled the *pampa* out

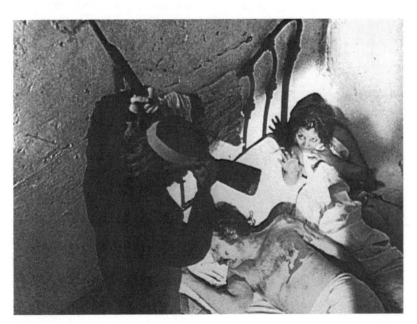

Juan Moreira

to themselves in huge tracts, reached a development protocol with British capital: the British would control all aspects of developing the country's transportation, industrial, and financial sectors, while the oligrachy would profit from bringing virgin *pampa* land into production and from the extremely high rent differentials the land offered once in production.* This arrangement endured for decades, leaving to British capital the ownership and control of the most critical sectors of the modern Argentine economy. So assiduously was this protocol observed that the country's first rail line into the *pampa*, though built with Argentine capital, was sold to the British. The latter, meanwhile, sold British parts and equipment to their own railroads at prices considerably higher than their European competitors' products, paid taxes in Britain but not in Argentina, and generally maintained the lines so poorly that when Perón nationalized them in 1948 the British were glad to see them go.

Nevertheless, at the turn of the century, Argentina was experiencing a phenomenal growth rate under this arrangement and was modernizing more quickly than any other Latin American country. As the continent's most industrialized and prosperous country, with one of the world's highest per-capita incomes, Argentina was seen as a model of Latin American development. But of course this was a development strategy that mortgaged the country's future to British capital. Any industry that might have threatened British exports to Argentina — from textiles to heavy machinery — was not allowed to develop. The extent of British holdings in Argentina at the time was staggering: prior to the First World War, fully one-half of all foreign investment in Latin America was in Argentina, where Britain was by far the largest investor.

Argentina's population problem was solved by turning to a different region of Europe. Massive immigration from Central and Southern Europe, and especially from Italy, led to a four-fold increase in the country's population between 1880 and 1914, to some eight million people. By 1914 about one-half of the country's population was first generation immigrant; over one million arrived in the first decade of the century alone.

* A rent differential is the term applied to the profits that accrue from higher agricultural yields than the average because of the fertility of the soil or advanced farming techniques.

Although Argentina's economy in those years was similar to Canada's, based on the export of primary agricultural goods, quite dissimilar patterns of population settlement grew up in the two countries. The existence of an oligarchical class in Argentina, with its vast land holdings, prevented the rise of an Anglo-Saxon family farm settlement pattern. Because beef production, the primary activity on the *pampa*, required relatively little labour, and grain harvests were carried out largely by seasonal European labourers, most of the country's immigrants settled in urban centres. Argentina is thus unique in Latin America for its lack of a rural peasantry. These immigrants brought to Argentina the strong anarcho-syndicalist union tradition that had arisen in Europe at the turn of the century, and quickly organized a radical and active working class movement in Argentina's urban centres. They also brought with them to Argentina a love of the new European artform of moving pictures.

Newspaper ad for El último malón *(The Last Indian Uprising), 1918*

The Argentine Silent Film: 1897-1931

The rapid growth and popularity of Argentine cinema in the silent period was conditioned by many factors. A radical working class with popular European cultural roots was formed simultaneously with the first Argentine experiments in film production, at a time when cinema was an exclusively proletarian entertainment. The Argentine economy was as developed as that of Canada or Southern Europe. The print mass media flourished, accompanied by the continent's highest literacy rate. The emerging domestic film market enjoyed a relative autonomy, before concerted U.S. efforts to monopolize foreign markets and smother national film industries. Under these conditions, film grew rapidly in Argentina in the silent period, peaking in the boom period of 1915-21, during which 100 features were made.

Despite the inevitable influence of foreign innovations on the nascent Argentine film industry, and the preponderance of first generation European immigrant talent working in it, the films of this early period reveal a great interest in national themes. They also benefitted from a close collaboration between filmmakers and other national artists, including novelists, visual artists, and musicians. It is worth noting that the pioneer immigrant directors adapted Argentine history and popular culture to the screen from the industry's very beginnings. Mario Gallo, an Italian who arrived in the country in 1905, directed the country's first dramatic film, *El fusilamiento de Dorrego* (Dorrego's Execution) in 1909, and went on to make a series of other dramatizations of Argentine history, including *La Revolución de mayo* (The May Revolution), *La batalla de Maipú* (The Battle at Maipú), and the first of many interpretations of the life of the famous *gaucho*, *Juan Moreira*. As the country was being inundated with immigrants in these years (many of whom kept their original citizenships and considered themselves, at least at first, as working visitors), a popular film culture developed that drew on Argentina's cultural heritage and later explored the lives of the country's working classes. The most successful film of the silent period, *Nobleza gaucha* (Gaucho Nobility, by Eduardo Martínez de la Pera, Ernesto Gunch, and Humberto Cairo, 1915) — made just one year after production of the country's first dramatic feature, *Amalia*, by Enrique García Velloso — is an example of this. Its *gaucho* theme was developed by the use of inter-titles taken from José Fernández's classic of *gaucho* poetry, *Martín Fierro* (1872), one of the most significant and influential texts in Argentine literature. The film also contained sequences shot in Buenos Aires, showing daily life there as well. Its huge popularity, in Argentina and throughout the Hispanic world, was instrumental in creating a public for Argentine films.

At the same time Argentine cinema, in keeping with the traditions of the country's popular culture, began to examine national political life with characteristic humour and frankness. In 1917, one of the great pioneers of Argentine cinema, Federico Valle, who had studied under Georges Méliès in Europe, produced the world's first feature-length animation film, *El apóstol* (The Apostle), directed by Quirino Cristiani, Diógenes Taborda, and Andrés Decaud. A satire of the Radical President Hipólito Yrigoyen, it was distinguished by its depiction of Buenos Aires and its use of local idioms. That same

President Hipólito Yrigoyen, as he appears in El apóstol

year, the anthropologist Alcides Greca shot the full-length *El último malón* (the Last Indian Uprising), which was part documentary of the scandalous living conditions of natives in the province of Santa Fé, and part re-enactment of an uprising they had staged in 1904, using the natives as actors playing themselves. In 1919, two films were made in response to the brutal repression of the workers' movement known as *la Semana Tragica*, the Tragic Week, during which police battled workers in the streets in a final, and largely successful, attempt to end the country's labour unrest and rid the unions of their anarcho-syndicalist elements. The first film was *Juan sin ropa* (Juan Without Clothes), a dramatization of the event, directed by the Frenchman Georges Benoît and produced by the prolific Camila and Héctor Quiroga. The second, *La semana tragica*, was a documentary filmed by Pío Quadro. While increasing political repression was leading to workers being beaten in the streets, it was not preventing filmmakers from recording the event.

José Augustin Ferreyra, despite his unusual talents, achievements, and working methods, can in many ways be considered

Federico Valle's photographic equipment supply store, Buenos Aires, 1919

representative of the talent at work in the young national cinema. A mulatto painter, set designer, and song lyricist, Ferreyra, like many of his contemporaries, worked in film while keeping up his other artistic pursuits, and often applied these in his films. He reportedly refused to work with scripts or see

José Augustin Ferreyra

other people's films, but still he made some of the country's most significant films in his 25-year career. His background and approach in these early years, however, were typical in the industry. Film producers were artisans, not industrialists; there were no established studios with regular production schedules or personnel. As I have mentioned, many of the directors came to film from other disciplines and incorporated their other work into their films, collaborating as well with some of Argentina's leading novelists during this period rich in literary output. In *La muchacha de Arrabal* (The Girl from Arrabal or The Girl from the Slums, 1922), Ferreyra wrote the lyrics to the tango that accompanied the film, the first live musical accompaniment in Argentine cinema. Films were often the result of an artistic collaboration, rather than the work of one director: *Nobleza gaucha* was the collaborative effort of Martinez de la Pera, Gunch, and Cairo, who shared directorial and technical credits.

It was an industry with great intellectual ferment, but it was also erratic and unstable. Apart from a few of the better films, most were not profitable (although *Nobleza gaucha* returned 600,000 pesos to its producers, from an investment of 20,000). This economic instability would prove disastrous in the post-war period, when the U.S. began its drive to cover the globe with its films.

1923 edition of sheet music from La muchacha del arrabal

José Augustin Ferreyra (centre)

Just as Argentina was developing its new-born feature film industry in 1914-15, war in Europe brought film production there to a halt and opened foreign markets to other film industries. *Nobleza gaucha* introduced Argentine films to these markets, and the Argentine film production boom of 1915-21 was fueled in part by these foreign sales. Argentina's film industry quickly became an export-oriented industry, sustaining production at higher levels than its small domestic market would normally support. (It has remained an industry whose economic health has depended on international sales. Today the Argentine domestic market, numerically, is less than one-third the size of Brazil's and one-half the size of Mexico's).

1920 brought a return to more normal production levels in Europe and a concerted international marketing offensive by the U.S. industry, after it emerged from the chaos of the new trust wars in the teens. Argentina, the most prosperous and industrialized Latin American country, and with one of the largest and most developed film markets, was a major target in this U.S. drive to penetrate foreign markets. One of the first changes was the establishment of direct distribution subsidiaries for U.S. films in each foreign market, funneling rental profits directly back to the U.S. producers. Argentine distributors, who had previously handled U.S. films and had come to rely on their revenue, were cut out of the picture. As the 1920s progressed, Argentine production progressively fell while U.S. imports rose; the country was soon the second largest importer of U.S. films (after Australia and before Brazil). By the end of the decade, when the national industry had become nearly paralyzed, national films accounted for only 10% of the domestic box-office and foreign markets had been lost. Only the introduction of sound technology would be able to reverse the industry's fortunes.

Publicity for Muñequitas porteñas *(Port Dolls)*

The Golden Years of the Argentine Sound Film: 1931-1942

In 1927, in the midst of the crisis affecting the Argentine film industry, Ferreyra began an international tour with his films. They were well received abroad, but sales were not as good as he had hoped. He returned to Argentina, however, innoculated with the growing world-wide interest in sound technology. In 1931, following other filmmakers' experiments with sound in the production of short films, Ferreyra directed the country's first sound feature, *Muñequitas porteñas* (Port Dolls), using discs. Two years later, the first Latin American optical sound studios were built and the optical sound features *Tango* (Luis Moglia Barth) and *Los tres berretines* (The Three Whims, by Enrique Susini) were shot. The next decade saw the consolidation of the Argentine film industry as the continent's largest and most successful. Film became the major form of entertainment for the Argentine working classes and extensive foreign markets throughout the Hispanic world were re-opened to Argentine filmmakers.

The use of sound in Argentine film ended the near absolute dominance of U.S. films in the domestic market, not only because the public could now hear dialogue in the peculiar Argentine Spanish *rioplatense* dialect, but because Argentine filmmakers quickly moved to incorporate elements of national culture into their films. The tango film is the best example of this: it was the largest and most distinctively Argentine genre of the period. It was also very popular abroad, demonstrating that foreign audiences didn't mind seeing Argentine culture on their movie screens. Sound gave the film industry a new capacity to infuse the country's vigorous popular culture into its works, creating a uniquely Argentine cinema with selling power abroad.

The implications of the introduction of sound technology into foreign film industries was not lost on U.S. producers who, more out of concern for their European markets than their Latin American ones, began producing films in two languages (*Der Blauer Angel* — The Blue Angel, by Joseph von Sternberg, is perhaps the most famous example of this tactic). They also began production of cheap foreign language films aimed at specific foreign markets. Studios were established in Hollywood and in Joinville, France for the production of Spanish-language films. Most of the technicians were from Spain and, for the most part, the films were more popular there than in Latin America. When this was realized, along with the fact that U.S. sales abroad had not diminished as much as had been feared, these productions were abandoned.

Tango, *by Luis Moglia Barth, 1933*

Because of these factors, the Argentine film industry was able to grow rapidly throughout the 1930s, reaching a peak production of 56 films in 1942, and creating a working class audience for its films alongside the U.S. imports in Argentina and throughout Latin America.

An important component of this audience for Argentine films was Argentine women. In an era before television, when movie theatres were showing very long programs (four or five films for one very low admission price), Argentine women made film-going a regular social activity. A number of film genres developed in order to service this market, especially comedies and dramas that featured women in lead roles (*Mujeres que trabajan* — Working Women, by Manuel Romero, 1938, is an example of a comedy in this vein). Some of the country's best directors worked in the genre, including Romero and Ferreyra, who made films such as *La que no perdonó* (She Who Didn't Forgive, 1936) and *La ley que olvidaron* (The Law They Forgot, 1938) with the box-office attraction Libertad Lamarque. The genre and the social practices it engendered seem to me worthy of a full cinematic and sociological enquiry, that might take as its starting points a thematic comparison between these films and present-day Argentine daytime television, and a study of the social relations between women that were forged by this regular movie-going habit.

The year 1937 marked a turning point in the development of Argentine cinema. Production that year was 28 features, climbing until it peaked at 56 in 1942, when the industry began its rapid decline. This brief five-year period can be considered something of a golden age for Argentine cinema, characterized by high levels of production; increasing technical quality, especially with the founding of the *Alex* labs in 1937; a wide diversity of genres; and such success in foreign markets that inroads were being made into the U.S. Hispanic market.

Of the many film genres to emerge in this period, the most significant was that known as the "social-folkloric." Following a tradition of urban realism developed primarily by Ferreyra (e.g. *Calles de Buenos Aires* — Streets of Buenos Aires, 1935) the social-folkloric genre shifted attention to rural or historical themes, combining an implicit social criticism with a depiction of either historical events or contemporary rural

life in a very popular entertainment cinema. This genre, without equal in the region's other film industries in Mexico and Brazil, was inaugurated by Mario Soffici in 1938 with the film *Kilómetro 111*, about the social conflicts that arise when the railroad comes to a rural area. Soffici contributed the best example of the genre a year later, *Prisioneros de la tierra* (Prisoners of the Earth). The historical films drew on a long tradition of *gaucho* literature and film. *La guerra gaucha* (The Gaucho War), made by Lucas Demare in 1942, was the most nationalistic of these. It was the first film to be produced by the new production company *Artistas Argentinos Asociados*, formed a year earlier by a group of young nationalists, and depicts the *gauchos* as the true defenders of Argentina's new independence against Spanish attacks.

It would be a mistake to attribute to this genre, or to any other being produced in Argentina at this time, a radical break

La guerra gaucha

Poster for Prisioneros de la tierra, *by Argentine painter Osvaldo M. Venturi*

Fuera de la ley *(Outlaw)*

with the dominant form of U.S. entertainment cinema. Regarding Soffici's *Prisioneros de la tierra*, the critic Domingo di Núbila noted the influence of John Ford, and remarked that the film was "national, but not nationalistic; Argentine, but not gauchesque; and typical, without being stereotypical." A top director of the time was Manuel Romero, whose films reveal the strong influence of Hollywood genres. His comedies, such as *La rubia del camino* (The Blonde en Route, 1938) show the influence of Frank Capra. Romero also made the first Argentine gangster film, *Fuera de la ley* (Outlaw, 1937). But while Argentine cinema at this time was modeled on the dominant U.S. forms, it dealt with specifically Argentine themes and, in the case of the social-folkloric and urban realism genres, depicted Argentine history and contemporary rural and working class life in a critical manner.

This attempt to develop a distinct national cinema — and especially to establish a socially critical genre within its mainstream — was a tentative one that lasted little more than a decade. That its social criticism was implicit and not explicit was a result not only of censorship and commercial pressures but

of the fact that these films predated the rebirth of a radical
nationalism, with a modern class perspective, that came with
the election of Perón in 1946. In 1973, when the film industry
next got a chance to return to the project of synthesizing
popular national culture and social criticism (there would be
no such opportunity during Perón's first presidencies, for
reasons I will discuss below), the social criticism had been made
explicit by years of struggle against military rule. This project's
success in the 1970s was made possible by a short-lived
rapprochement between the country's middle and working
classes, while the project of 1931-42 was abandoned because
of a widening gulf between the two.

The Decline of the Argentine Film Industry: 1942-1955

From about 1942, several diverse factors converged to bring
about the swift decline of the Argentine film industry. These
can be identified as: 1) U.S. political and cultural initiatives
in Latin America during the war; 2) the management of the
Argentine film industry, combined with, after 1944, the effects
of legislative attempts to halt its decline; and 3) fundamental
changes in the artistic priorities and social perspective of the
film industry's creative talent. I will consider each of these
factors in turn.

1) U.S. Foreign Policy in Latin America During the War.

By 1942 (and until 1944) Argentina had maintained its
neutrality in World War Two, and was the only country in
the hemisphere that continued to have trade and diplomatic
relations with the Axis powers. Not long before, Brazil had
broken its pledge of neutrality, under intense pressure from
the United States. Argentina, however, was determined not
to do so, particularly after the installation of a pro-Axis
military government under General Pedro Ramírez in 1943.
Much has been made of fascist elements in the Argentine ruling
class of this time (which were in sympathy with similar tendencies amongst an influential minority in the Allied countries, particularly in Britain and France), but it is important to note that
the U.S. dispute with Argentina over the latter's insistence on

neutrality was not prompted simply by the former's belief that fascism must be opposed, particularly as the U.S. was itself a latecomer to this cause. Instead, the dispute must be seen in the context of U.S. ambitions for hemispheric hegemony, which were formulated about this time. Argentina's independent foreign policy was an intolerable affront that stood in the way of these ambitions. This was one reason that Britain, for instance, supported Argentina's claim to neutrality (the Roosevelt-Churchill correspondence reveals that this issue was one of the most bitter disagreements the two had). Fearing for the future of its own influence in the region after the inevitable post-war political and economic realignments, Britain curried favour in Buenos Aires by supporting the Argentine claim to neutrality. It was also motivated by a real concern for the safety of food shipments from Argentina to Britain during the war; these

Publicity for Kilómetro 111, by Mario Soffici, 1938

Argentina Sono Film publicity in La Nación, *March 27, 1938. The heading reads "Be patriotic! See Argentine films!"*

would be most secure if shipped under a neutral flag.

Unable to intimidate the Argentine government into abandoning its neutrality, and concerned that visible pro-Axis elements in Argentine society might somehow turn to the production of pro-Axis propaganda, the U.S. imposed a total embargo on raw film stock shipments to the country. Predictably, the industry was paralyzed. A black market in raw stock was born, supplied by neighbouring countries with ample stocks. Virtually all of the smaller Argentine film production companies closed, leaving only the three or four largest producers in business. Production fell from 56 films in 1942 to 23 films in 1945. There was very little raw stock available for the production of prints for foreign sales. The Argentine film industry had been sabotaged.

The U.S. claimed, in announcing the embargo, that it feared Argentina becoming a centre of Spanish-language pro-Axis propaganda production. While this concern was sincerely held in some circles, it must be qualified by two points. The first is the extreme unlikelihood that the Argentine film industry, or the Argentine government, had the desire to undertake such a task. Secondly, it must be noted that a partial embargo continued until after Argentina's pro-Allied reversal in 1944, and even after 1945, indicating motives other than those given. The embargo must therefore be seen in light of the U.S.'s long-term political and cultural objectives in Latin America.

Although it is true that Nazi Germany had made some Spanish-language propaganda films, that Spain had made some pro-Axis films, and that the German Embassy in Buenos Aires was a source of pro-Axis literature during the war, it was a different matter altogether to assume that the Argentine film industry was about to put pro-Axis films into production in 1942. Throughout the 1930s and 40s, not only was Argentine cinema the most visibly democratic of all the national mass media, it was also the most visibly democratic cinema in Latin America. The first Latin American pro-Allied film, *V enfrenta Blitzkrieg* (V Confronts Blitzkrieg) was made in Argentina in 1941, before Pearl Harbour. Argentine film talent regularly spoke out against the government's neutrality, indicating that they were unlikely to begin pro-Axis propaganda production on their own initiative. Nor was the government in much of a position to induce such a change in direction (it is important to remember that the Argentine government became openly pro-Axis only after the coup of 1943, *after* the imposition of the embargo). There were simply no interventionist mechanisms the government could have relied upon in order to do so. There was no state funding of the industry, no formal censorship process of Argentine films (although Charlie Chaplin's *The Great Dictator* had been refused entry into the country in 1940*), and no state involvement in distribution or exhibition. In any event, in 1942 there was no indication of any intent on the part of the industry or the government to put pro-Axis films into production, and the predictable ruin of the industry that resulted from the embargo might have given the U.S. pause and encouraged a more wait-and-see attitude. Instead, it was the ruin of the Argentine film industry that had spurred them on.

In 1941, the three largest U.S. film companies operating in Argentina posted a combined revenue of around 1,200,000 *pesos* ($300,000 U.S.). The total earnings of the two largest Argentine producers that year, *Argentina Sono Film* and *Lumiton*, were 3,500,000 *pesos*. That same year, Paramount's chief in Buenos Aires reported to Nelson Rockefeller's Office of the Coordinator of Inter American Affairs (CIAA) that the success of Argentine films was threatening U.S. sales in Latin America. Since the failure of Hollywood's Spanish-language productions in the mid-thirties, the U.S. had been distributing its films in Latin America in English with Spanish subtitles. This tactic had failed to capture the large working class market there. The Argentine films were more popular because of the intrinsic appeal of spoken Spanish, the region's widespread illiteracy, and a closer cultural identification with indigenous production. However, when the outbreak of war virtually closed European film markets, U.S. producers began to look at the

* It is worth noting that the film was also banned in several U.S. juridictions, including the city of Chicago, and that Chaplin was subpoenaed to testify before the House Committee on Interstate Commerce's enquiry into Motion Picture Propaganda. Chaplin never appeared before the Committee, however, because the U.S. entry into the war rendered obsolete the complaint that *The Great Dictator* was "prematurely anti-fascist."

Latin American market with renewed interest.

In a move to increase their sales to the region, the U.S. industry began to produce films with Latin themes. In 1943, it was announced that twenty-five such films were in production; thirty had already been made since the outbreak of the war. Latin film stars and talent were brought to Hollywood to "latinize" production. Carmen Miranda, the "Brazilian Bombshell" was the most famous of these. U.S. filmmakers also visited Latin America: both Orson Welles and Walt Disney went south on behalf of the CIAA. Welles shot *It's All True* on location in Brazil, an RKO-CIAA co-production with Nelson Rockefeller credited as Executive Producer. The film was never completed or released, however, owing to disputes between Welles and RKO. Disney's 1941 tour resulted in two Spanish-language films made on his return to the U.S.: *Saludos amigos*, in 1942; and *Los tres caballeros* (The Three Gents) in 1943. The latter, part live-action with Carmen Miranda and part animation with Donald Duck, broke attendance records in Mexico City.

It soon became apparent that this was only the first stage of a far-reaching U.S. cultural offensive in Latin America. When Rockefeller's Office of the Coordinator of Inter American Affairs was founded in 1940, it soon formed a Motion Picture Division. Its members, like Rockefeller, had personal and financial ties to Hollywood (the Division's first Director, John Hay Whitney, was vice-president of the Museum of Modern

Libertad Lamarque sings for Orson Welles. Left to right: director Alberto de Zavalía; Lamarque; the wife of the U.S. ambassador; Welles. 1942

Art and director of its film library; he also financed production of *Gone With the Wind*). At first, the CIAA's role was limited to promoting the new U.S. Latin-themed films in Latin America and to acting as a goodwill ambassador between Hollywood and Latin America; encouraging U.S. producers, for example, to treat their Latin themes and characters with more sensitivity. With the U.S. entry into the war in 1942, a Newsreel Division was established to produce and distribute pro-Ally propaganda in Latin America. This led to a general assessment of distribution and production sectors in Latin America, and it was a few months afterwards that the CIAA was recommending an embargo on raw film stock shipments to Argentina. Later that same year, the CIAA spearheaded a veritable flood of U.S. capital investment into the Mexican film industry that belied the true motive for the embargo.

When the embargo was first imposed in 1942, Mexico's film production was substantially less than Argentina's, with an output of 42 films that year compared to Argentina's 56. In addition, the quality of Mexican films was decidedly inferior, and they were not nearly as popular in the Latin American markets. Since the 1930s, several U.S. investors had acquired considerable interests in Mexican production and distribution companies and movie theatre chains. This investment in the Mexican film industry was encouraged by the CIAA after the imposition of the embargo on the Argentine industry. The CIAA also approved huge increases in Mexican raw stock allotments (at a time of shortages in the U.S.), equipment sales, and technical assistance. For example, by 1945 RKO (linked to Rockefeller money) had acquired 49% of the *Churubuscu* studios (only Mexican foreign investment laws prevented them from acquiring more). Columbia had extensive investments as well, and the entrepreneur William Jenkins controlled a 22-movie theatre chain that included some of Mexico City's best cinemas. His holdings were so extensive that in the 1950s he was accused of controlling the Mexican film industry. As a result of this intensive investment, in tandem with the effects of the embargo placed on the Argentine film industry, the positions of Mexico and Argentina in the Latin American market were reversed by 1945. The U.S. had conceded the necessity, or inevitability, of indigenous film production in Latin America. Extensive investments in the Mexican film industry ensured that this production would nevertheless be profitable to U.S. interests. It also ensured the ideological dependability of Latin American film production, a concern not limited to the possible production of pro-Axis propaganda during the war.

2) The Management of the Argentine Film Industry

When the raw stock embargo hit the Argentine film industry in 1942, it precipitated another crisis that had been brewing within the industry throughout the sound period. Though Argentine films were far superior technically and artistically to Mexican films, the Argentine film industry was indisputably mismanaged in comparison. This mismanagement was visible on the three critical levels of production methods, international distribution and domestic distribution. In each instance, the Mexican film industry — aided by an interventionist Mexican government — was managed with far more foresight and acumen than was the Argentine industry. Mexican initiatives in each of these three critical sectors came about in the late 1930s, positioning the industry for the takeover of Latin American film markets in the 1940s, aided by the U.S.

As late as 1942, Argentine producers were still making films in an anachronistic studio system, which kept film workers on the payroll year round, whether they were working or not. The Mexicans, by that date, had converted to a crew system that, in addition to cutting labour costs, enabled them to shoot a feature in half the time it took Argentine producers. The Mexican government also established a *Banco Cinematográfico*, to provide production loans, a decade before a similar program was set up in Argentina under Perón. The Mexican approach to foreign sales also showed more foresight and again benefitted from government intervention. An international sales agency, *Pel-Mex*, was set up with state assistance to promote Mexican films abroad. The Argentine industry, lacking a centralized sales agency, used a variety of sales agents in foreign markets. Argentine producers took no percentages from these agents, leasing the films instead at a flat fee, and the truth is that throughout the period of the great success of Argentine films abroad, very little revenue was actually being returned to their producers.

Argentine producers had an even more acute revenue problem in their domestic market. As late as 1941, Argentina had the world's longest running film programs: four or five features running seven hours or more could be seen for one *peso* (25¢ U.S.). The domestic market in the years preceding the embargo was consumed by an exhibitors' price war. Some exhibitors would rent films, with no intention of showing them, simply to keep them out of competitors' hands. That they could afford to do so gives a good indication of what they were paying Argentine producers for their films. The Mexican industry, in contrast, had halved its program lengths in 1935. By the end of the decade, Mexican domestic box-office revenues had increased from 40-50% of Argentina's to some 70-90%. The Argentine producers during this same period were locked into sales agreements with the country's exhibitors that, like their arrangements with the foreign sales agents, returned little money to them. The films were leased to exhibitors for flat rates; if a film was successful, the exhibitor, and not the producer, benefitted. During this period of great domestic popularity, therefore, not enough money was being returned to the production sector to provide for sufficient capital

Advertisement for Petit Splendid *cinema, 1939*

investment in the industry.

In 1943, when the raw stock embargo was threatening to ruin the industry, the producers appealed to the new military government for legislative protection. Relations between the producers and the exhibitors were by now extremely acrimonious, and the government turned the political hot potato over to the new Secretary of Labour and Social Welfare, Col. Juan Domingo Perón. One year later, Perón introduced the first legislation affecting the country's film industry, which imposed a scale of rental percentages on the exhibitors and, to their further horror, a minimum quota on the exhibition of national films as well. These exhibition quotas, curiously enough, required that more Argentine films be exhibited than were actually produced — ensuring, if nothing else, their stimulating effect: by 1950, production matched the peak of 56 films that had last been attained in 1942.

Inevitably, however, investment adventurers flocked to the film industry, attracted by the notion that every film produced was virtually guaranteed exhibition under the law. This problem was exacerbated in 1947 when Perón (now a General, and President, following a landslide election victory in 1946) brought in legislation introducing a system of "A" and "B" classifications. Although "A" films, by virtue of their special artistic interest or national theme or source, were actually guaranteed obligatory exhibition, "B" films received a larger percentage of their budgets from a state production assistance fund. Cheaper films thus became more advantageous to make than better, more expensive films. This gave rise to the production of "quickies": cheap, poor quality films that lacked the social criticism or even the realistic treatment of everyday Argentine life of the popular cinema of the late 1930s and early 1940s.

In addition to his legislative initiatives to protect Argentine cinema through exhibition quotas and production assistance, Perón moved to control the supply of foreign films in the domestic market. Import quotas were imposed that led to a great reduction in the number of U.S. films seen in Argentina (reaching a low of 131 films in 1950, not coincidentally the year of the highest domestic production under Perón). There can be no doubt that these initiatives of production assistance and import and exhibition quotas were largely responsible for keeping the Argentine film industry alive when, left to market forces, it would have surely collapsed under the weight of the U.S. offensive in Latin American cultural markets and, as we shall see, from the effects of the national industry's anti-popular production strategies of the 1940s. At the same time, the industry was hampered by the corrupt Peronist bureaucracy, which controlled raw film stock allocations, and by Perón's personal and political vendettas against some of the industry's creative talent, creating a flow of exiles and self-exiles out of Argentina during his rule.

But above all, Perón sought, in what might be argued a cynical and short-sighted way, to keep the tradition of a popular national cinema alive. He refused, for example, to raise cinema admission prices throughout his decade in power, despite very high inflation rates. By 1955, Argentina had admission prices among the lowest in the world; perhaps *the* lowest when considered against per capita income. This tactic, however, like the other initiatives described above (apart from the important intervention in the dispute over film

Luis Saslavsky, photographed by Annemarie Heinrich, 1940

rental rates), was a stop-gap measure that did little to address the structural problems facing the industry. One of these was the need for international sales, something that was neglected by Perón. Nor was the "popular" cinema that was produced under his rule, the "B" quickies, anything more than a shell of the cinema that was produced in the pre-1942 era. The vitality and diversity of themes were lost in an industry protected by exhibition quotas and debased by the emphasis on cheap productions.

It was under Perón's rule — although it was certainly not entirely his doing — that popular cinema became "Mexicanized," or ghettoized into cheap productions that no longer occupied a central place in the industry or attracted its best talent.

Nevertheless, Perón's legacy must be seen in the context not only of foreign interests that would have been quite content to see the demise of the Argentine film industry (and were doing what they could to hasten this) but of a national industry whose top talents had renounced the popular themes of the 1930s in favour of a bourgeois European aesthetic.*

Not only did this strategy have disastrous commercial repercussions in an industry that relied heavily on an Argentine and Latin American working class public, but it came, ironically, at the time of the working class's greatest political and economic triumphs under Perón.

3) The Artistic Decline of the Argentine Film Industry

Signs of artistic decay actually appeared in the Argentine film industry in the late 1930s, when it was enjoying its greatest popular success. While most of the industry was oriented towards the production of working class entertainment, some sectors began concentrating on a smaller national middle class market. By 1942, precisely at the time of the stock embargo and the crises of domestic and international distribution, this trend had begun to further threaten the success of Argentine films. This change in the thematic and stylistic orientation of the industry must be seen in the context of the growth of a middle class from the ranks of the country's second gener-

---

* After Perón's overthrow in 1955, one filmmaker is said to have remarked proudly "we didn't make one pro-Peronist film during his rule."

Libertad Lamarque in Besos Brujos *(Magic Kisses), by José A. Ferreyra, 1937*

ation immigrant population as the Argentine capitalist economy matured.

Film historian Domingo di Núbila cites 1940 as the key date in this transformation. It is significant that he attributes the decline directly to the class origin of a new generation of filmmakers who "didn't live in lodging-houses, use public transit, or wear ordinary clothes — directors who didn't participate in popular life the way filmmakers used to." Informed not by the populist approach of the generation of the 1930s, but by a personalized approach that valued "artistic innovation" over working within the national tradition, and linked more to European culture than to Latin American or national culture, these directors transposed the "civilization vs. barbarism" conflict onto modern Argentina's most popular and nationalistic culture industry.

The work of the director Luis Saslavsky illustrates the dynamics of this conflict. No doubt one of the more talented directors to appear in the late 1930s, his mature work in the 1940s oscillated between Europeanized and static formal experiments and a more realistic style in the national tradition. In 1939 he was asked to work with the country's biggest female box-office attraction, the singer Libertad Lamarque. Lamarque had just finished a trilogy of films with Ferreyra that were among the most popular of the decade, and firmly in the tradition of the popular musicals that played such an important role in the development of a national style in the early sound years. Saslavsky reportedly hadn't seen these or any other Lamarque films when he was asked to work with her, something that is not only hard to imagine but also an indication of what was to come of their collaboration. *La casa del recuerdo* (The House of Memory, 1940), with Lamarque, was a box office disaster, the realism and populism of Ferreyra having been abandoned for a new "European" formalism ("sterile aestheticism," di Núbila wrote).

This change in direction was conditioned, as I mentioned above, by changes underway in Argentine society, as well as in the film industry itself. Argentine cinema, like many national cinemas in the early sound period, was undergoing a consolidation that saw it become less sporadic and artisanal and more capital-intensive. At the same time, the Argentine labour movement throughout the 1930s became less active and less militant, suffering under the repression of *la decada infame* and not yet reoriented to the realities of the country's intensive industrialization and to the growth of a lower middle class. In the context of this decline in the vigor of working class political life, and under social and economic pressure from a new middle class, the film industry in Argentina gradually shed its uniquely proletarian character. This same strategy met with great success elsewhere, most notably in the U.S., where films aimed at the middle class brought new patrons into the previously immigrant and working class movie theatres. In Argentina, however, this approach was fatal. The social and economic changes described above were not nearly as pronounced or extensive there as they were in the U.S. The country's population in 1940 was about fifteen million people, indicating in real terms how large the bourgeois market for film was, whatever the new visibility and influence of a national middle class. Even the working class market, as we have seen, was not large enough to sustain production at the high levels reached during the golden age (this had spurred the turn to foreign markets, and when these markets failed to remit adequate revenue, this too had become a factor in the decline in

La dama duende, *by Luis Saslavsky, 1945*

La dama de compañia *(The Lady in Waiting), by Alberto de Zavalía, 1940*

production). There can be no doubt, moreover, that Argentina had secured large foreign markets for its films, in direct competition with the U.S., because of the films' Latin American themes, which at that time were in demand in the region. With the turn to a "sterile aestheticism" and to European sources and themes, Argentine cinema no longer met the demand for a regional cinema in tune with Latin American working class culture. Di Núbila cites reports from the Argentine producers' foreign sales agents in 1943 warning that Argentine films were "losing touch" with the foreign market. It was a warning that went unheeded.

The stylistic and thematic turnaround in Argentine cinema during this period occurred on many levels. As an example of an early change, a few directors in the late 1930s began using the informal second person pronoun *tú* in their films instead of *vos*. The latter is a uniquely Argentine locution that is used almost universally there, crossing class lines, and heard virtually nowhere else in the Hispanic world. Its use had not hindered foreign sales, further proof that Argentine producers needn't have feared a characteristically national cinema. This curious move to the use of *tú*, then, is without logical explanation. It was as if by abandoning *vos* a deliberate attempt was being made to denationalize the national cinema.

Outdoor locations — images of the Argentine interior and of the city streets — were another victim of this new aesthetic, as more and more studio work was done. It was in these studios that the new genres of the 1940s were born, replacing the urban dramas and rural and *gaucho* epics so popular in the 1930s and early '40s. The bourgeois audience had always disdained the social dramas of that period, especially the social-folkloric genre. With the new production strategies of the 1940s, this genre, despite its popular and critical success, died a premature death in about 1942, four short years after its birth in 1938 with Soffici's *Kilómetro 111*. In its place a new generation of directors was producing everything from "white telephone" films, which showed a mythical bourgeoisie acting out insipid salon dramas in sanitized settings (hence the ubiquitous white telephone), to a new sort of historical film, shot largely in the studio, and based more often than not on European history.

A marked Europeanization of themes accompanied the stylistic transformation of the new films. A new generation of filmmakers was fulfilling Sarmiento's dream of a cultural tie with Europe, and not Latin America: "the young generation of Buenos Aires," Sarmiento had written nearly a century before, "took up this fruitful idea of a fraternity of interests with England and France, took up a love for the European people whose institutions and arts had given us civilization, which Rosas destroyed in the name of the Americas." Adaptations of Ibsen, Wilde, Chekhov, and Tolstoy — to name just a few of the European masters adapted to Argentine film screens — replaced the industry's former collaborations with Argentine writers. Foreign themes became the major sources for a new genre of "studio histories" that presented a static and stylized view of mostly European history. This move to foreign themes was so extreme that when Perón legislated in 1947 that 10% of all production be adapted from the work of national authors, foreign themes accounted for fully one-half of the industry's

Madame Bovary, *by Carlos Schlieper, 1947*

production.

The great irony, of course, is that this forceful turn from popular national themes and styles occurred during Perón's populist presidency. While its development predates Perón's entry into political life, and shouldn't be seen as a product of his rule, it must nevertheless be considered in the light of social antagonisms in Argentine society that Perón articulated and exacerbated. For example, Perón was elected President in 1946 with the massive support of the working class rank and file, but he initially did not have the support of the trade union hierarchy, which was justifiably suspicious of this pro-Axis populist. The print media were unanimously and actively hostile to his Presidency. The urban bourgeoisie did not like his social or labour reforms, or his corrupt bureaucracy, and viewed him as some sort of descendant of Rosas. His relationship with the film industry was essentially antagonistic. He first lost the support of the powerful exhibitors because of his intervention in their dispute with the producers. He later alienated many in the production sector with his personal and political campaigns against industry talent (Libertad Lamarque left the country during Perón's rule, for example, because of a feud with his actress wife Evita). However, these antagonisms do not explain a transformation such as the one the film industry underwent in the early 1940s. The reasons, once again, must be sought in the historic polarization of Argentina's social classes, a polarization which has always been a vivid part of the country's cultural life.

The Years of Military Rule and of the Third Peronist Presidency: 1955-1983

Space restrictions limit me to extremely cursory comments on the period after Perón's overthrow by the military in 1955, an event followed by the re-writing of film policy in 1957. Readers are referred to the articles by Fernando Birri, Octavio Getino, and Alfonso Gumucio Dagron, as well as to my own chronology of Argentine cinema elsewhere in this volume for a more complete picture of this period.

Two major trends appeared in — or, more precisely, in the margins of — the film industry in the late 1950s. While diametrically opposed thematically and stylistically, they shared, to varying degrees, persecution by the authorities and a rejection of the decayed mainstream of the industry. In 1956 Fernando Birri returned to Argentina from studies at the *Centro Sperimentale* in Rome to found *La Escuela Documental de Santa Fé*, a documentary film school. Two years later he produced the school's first film, *Tire dié* (Throw Me a Dime), cited by Julianne Burton as the first Latin American social documentary and revealing the visible influence of Birri's studies with the Italian neo-realists. Birri's cinema was both more critical and less "popular" than the cinema under discussion in this article; "less popular" in the sense that his films were generally not seen through normal commercial channels and were often censored. Birri's main influence, though immense, thus lies not in the production of critical films in the mainstream but in his work as a teacher, theorist, and documentarist of the country's social reality, particularly in the interior.

The other trend to appear in the late 1950s was a movement labelled the Argentine *nuevo cine*. Composed of a handful of young directors, this movement was influenced by the auteurist

Las aguas bajan turbias *(Troubled Waters)*

renewal underway in European cinema at the time. This intellectual and introverted style was transposed by the *nuevo cine* filmmakers onto an urban Argentina, resulting in a cinema with little in common with the genres of the 1930s. Although itself defined by a European style, *nuevo cine* was also a strong reaction against the work produced in the 1940s. "There are no white telephones in my films," declared Leopoldo Torre Nilsson, who is generally considered a key member of the movement, though his entry into the industry preceded the real birth of *nuevo cine* by a few years.

Not only did these filmmakers renounce the forms of the 1940s, they combined this new European style with a return to Argentine authors (albeit authors a world apart from a novelist such as Alfredo Varela, an Argentine communist whose *El río oscuro* was the source for the country's last great social-folkloric film, *Las aguas bajan turbias* (Troubled Waters, by Hugo del Carril, 1952). *Nuevo cine* directors adapted instead the urbane work of novelists such as Julio Cortázar, Beatriz Guido (Torre Nilsson's wife), and David Viñas.*

The birth of *Cine Liberación* in the late 1960s (a process Octavio Getino describes in detail elsewhere in these pages) was both a response to the state of the film industry in those years and a product of the social upheaval then underway in the country. At that time, the Argentine film industry, heavily censored since the end of a brief return to democracy in 1963, was composed of a thoroughly lifeless mainstream and a vigorous auteurist rump that was only beginning to produce features regularly, having long been marginalized. Neither the mainstream nor *nuevo cine* addressed themselves with any zeal to the political and social turbulence of the era. Perhaps this is due, on *nuevo cine's* part, to the censorship of quite innocuous films by two of its leading members, Manuel Antín and

---

* The later work of *nuevo cine* director Manuel Antín represents an exception to this trend. After early collaborations with Cortázar, (*La cifra impar* — The Odd Number, 1961), he turned to *gaucho* themes in the films *Don Segundo Sombra* (1969, from the national literary classic by Ricardo Güiraldes) and *Juan Manuel de Rosas* (1970). Leopoldo Torre Nilsson as well filmed *gaucho* themes during this period, including an adaptation of José Hernández's *Martín Fierro* (1968).

Fernando Ayala. The country's social turbulence was the result of the forging of an informal common front between the working and middle classes in a struggle against military rule. This process became particularly visible after 1969, a date that marked, not co-incidentally, *Cine Liberación's* issuance of their "Toward a Third Cinema" manifesto. In response to the political compromises required by auteurist production, and in the context of a growing acceptance of radical anti-imperialist theories by middle class intellectuals, *Cine Liberación* called for the creation of a "guerrilla cinema" that would join in the resistance. This cinema was based on principles of collective (and generally clandestine) production; parallel distribution, which involved audience discussion of the film; and unflinching political opposition to the military government. The group's first film, *La hora de los hornos* (The Hour of the Furnaces, by Fernando Solanas and Octavio Getino, 1966-68) was, as Getino reminds us, the first film to be used directly in the struggle for national liberation in a neo-colonized country.

For all *Cine Liberación's* revolutionary political rhetoric, it collaborated in the democratic process that began in 1973 with the abdication of the military and the return of Perón as President after eighteen years of exile. To the dismay of some

Left to right:
David Viñas, Fernando
Ayala, Héctor Olivera
circa 1957

elements of the Left in Argentina and abroad who were intoxicated with the notions of "permanent revolution" and "guerrilla cinema," *Cine Liberación* put down its arms, as it were, to join in a democratic process that we are tempted, in retrospect, to view as inherently flawed and doomed from the start. The group collaborated on two fronts: first, by assisting in the elaboration of film policy, primarily through the presence of Getino as director of the film classification board; and second, by renouncing clandestine *agit* film production and joining, more or less, the mainstream of the industry with a view to producing commercial films for general release.

There can be no doubt that on both counts the experience was fruitful. The elaboration of film policy during this third Peronist presidency was influenced more by the Peronist Left than were other social and economic policies. The abolition of censorship, the stimulation of production, and renewed efforts to limit the influence of foreign films in the domestic market all contributed to a cultural renaissance that benefitted from the participation of *Cine Liberación*.

In the context of a collective nostalgia for an imagined Argentine golden age (the affluent years of Perón's first presidency in the 1940s), the film industry undertook a

El familiar *(The Relative), by Octavio Getino, 1973*

Juan Moreira

remarkable revival of traditional Argentine film genres and themes. A number of important films were made by the country's best directors, films such as Olivera's *La Patagonia rebelde* (1974), Torre Nilsson's 1940s-style period piece "women's film" *Boquitas pintadas* (Painted Mouths, 1974), Leonardo Favio's *Juan Moreira* (1973) and Lautaro Murúa's *lumpen* drama *La Raulito* (Tomboy Paula, 1975). *Cine Liberación* directors contributed somewhat more radical visions of popular culture. Getino made *El familiar* (The Relative, 1973), financed by Italian television, based on a Tucumán legend. Fernando Solanas made *Los hijos de Fierro* (The Children of Fierro, 1972-77), a personal statement on the political events of the years of dictatorship and the success of the resistance movement. Gerardo Vallejo made *El Camino hacia la muerte del Viejo Reales* (Old Man Reales' Road to Death, 1970), a document of the three years he spent living with a rural family.

The course of political events after Perón's return is widely known. The national unity his return had promised, the unification of Argentina's polarized social classes behind a

La Raulito *(Tomboy Paula)*

populist leader, failed to take root. Following his death fourteen months after returning to power, the internal contradictions of Peronism exploded into increasingly violent confrontations between a radical Peronist Left, which had spearheaded the resistance movement, and right-wing cronies and union bosses from earlier days. An undeclared civil war began that was only intensified and given a name after the military took power in 1976. To the non-Peronist Left, the whole experience is offered today as proof not only of the internal contradictions that affected (and affect) Peronism, but of the inherent inadequacy of populism as a political strategy in the continuing struggle for national liberation and meaningful democracy. This view contains far-reaching implications for a film industry whose most critical and democratic elements, whether tied to Perón or not, have always followed an essentially populist course.

Los hijos de Fierro (*The Children of Fierro*), by Fernando Solanas, 1972-77

Film Under Democracy: 1983 to the present

I have already discussed, at the beginning of this article, some of the problems facing the Argentine film industry today after a decade of repression and economic chaos. The present composition of the industry is also discussed in some detail in the report prepared by *SICA* (the film workers' union) elsewhere in this volume. I will return here briefly to a discussion of some of these points in order to make a few tentative final comments on the future of Argentine cinema under democracy. Unfortunately, a proper consideration of the nature of that democracy lies well outside the scope of this book. It might be noted in passing, however, that President Raúl Alfonsín's Radical Party seems determined not to antagonize the military. Show trials of nine former Generals and Presidents have therefore taken the place of a thorough enquiry into the activities of the Armed Forces during the years of terror, and of the necessary structural reform of the military. Alfonsin has also distanced himself from the radical positions of, most notably, Peru and Cuba on the foreign debt question, and he has endeavoured to pay the Junta's US$55 billion debt on better terms than those sought by the IMF. This is having an enormous effect on living standards in Argentina and on the country's social services, as well as on indicators such as illiteracy, which has risen considerably in the last decade and continues to rise under democracy. All of these factors, as *SICA* points out in its report, are hindering the revival of the national film industry.

During the dictatorship, with the production and popularity of domestic films at an all-time low, Argentine distributors began to distribute large numbers of foreign films, particularly of course U.S. films (to an even larger extent than is "normal" in a neo-colonial cultural situation). Because of the Junta's censorship and the relatively low rates of return they offered, very few Latin American films were included among these. The distribution of Latin American films within the region has been problematic at the best of times, and in the past there have been proposals for the establishment of a Latin American common market for film.* This call has not been taken up in

* Proposed by, among others, the former head of *Embrafilme* in Brazil, Roberto Farias, and by Octavio Getino.

Argentina today, as sales priorities have been oriented away from the Latin American market, for reasons I will discuss. Nor have Argentine distributors rushed to put Latin American films on Argentine screens since the return of democracy: in the first half of 1985, only six Brazilian films, and no other Latin American films, opened commercially in the country. Because of the political censorship in Argentina for most of the past twenty years, Cuban cinema, for example, is virtually unknown there. It is only through the efforts of cine clubs and *SICA* seminars that it and other regional cinemas are seen at all. This activity, however, is obviously no replacement for mainstream distribution, the lack of which is perpetuating Argentina's cultural isolation from the rest of Latin America.*

After nearly a decade of dictatorship, Argentina's working class, traditionally the strongest market for national production, had become a relatively poor consumer of Argentine films. This remains true today, after nearly three years of democracy, and only partially because of Argentina's high per capita ownership of television sets or of the austerity measures of the present government, which include a wage freeze alongside 40% inflation, leaving little money in working class households for outings to the cinema. Film attendance in the working class districts of Buenos Aires and in the industrial cities of Córdoba and Rosario fell substantially in 1985 after rising in

---

* Further evidence of the inadequacy of the Argentine film distribution sector is provided by the recent case of Jean-Luc Godard's film *Je vous salue, Marie* (Hail Mary, 1985). This film, as is well known, has aroused considerable controversy around the world, been denounced by the Pope, and is banned in many countries, including the newly democratic Brazil. Brazil's President succumbed to intense Catholic pressure and banned the film over the protests of his censor board. Its future waˢ also hotly debated in Argentina, where the Catholic hierarchy may be even more conservative and powerful (many of the country's most powerful Church figures, for example, supported the Junta to the very end). Despite one prominent Catholic's claim that President Alfonsín personally assured him the film would not be allowed into the country, no such prohibition order followed. However, six months after the controversy, no Argentine distributor has bought the rights to it and it has not been seen in Argentina.

1984, the first year of democracy. While overall admissions to Buenos Aires movie theatres fell 6.1% between 1984 and 1985 (a startling and troublesome figure in itself), di Núbila, writing in *Variety**, cites unnamed industry sources as saying that this figure doesn't approach the "disastrous" drop in attendance in the working class districts. The problem today is not simply one of a lost movie-going habit compounded by an economic crisis that encourages people to stay home and watch TV. It is instead a result of a production strategy that emphasizes production for the national middle class and European markets while neglecting the national working class and Latin American markets.

In the production sector, the response to Argentina's historic dependence on foreign markets in order to maintain high levels of production has been to orient production to the lucrative West European and North American markets. This strategy has been vindicated by the success in these markets of such films as *Camila* (María Luisa Bemberg, 1984), *La historia oficial* (The Official Story, by Luis Puenzo, 1985) and *Tangos: el exilio de Gardel* (Tangos: the Exile of Gardel, by Fernando Solanas, 1985). In turn however, it has required the industry to virtually write off the Latin American market because of its fundamental incompatibility with the European market (I will discuss how Solanas' film represents an exception). Because of the Latin American debt crisis, government controls on foreign profit remittances, and widespread video piracy, to name just three of the problems currently affecting Latin American film industries, the present-day Latin American market offers few opportunities for substantial sales revenue. While the Argentine strategy is thus a response to the undeniable reality of film distribution in Latin America, it exacerbates at the same time the historic problem of the orientation of Argentine culture to European tastes. For this reason, the strategy is not without its detractors in Argentina today, who fear that an overriding concern with the success of Argentine films in the European market will eventually lead to a distortion of the national style. Already, it has visibly alienated the domestic working class market, as the best directors are now working

* *Variety*, 12 March 1986.

on prestigious productions aimed at foreign markets (the most notable examples of this in 1986 are Raúl de la Torre's *Pobre mariposa* (Poor Butterfly) and María Luisa Bemberg's *Miss Mary*. The latter was unfinished when I was in Argentina in May 1986, while the former had just gone into local release after representing the country in competition in Cannes. Primed as the prestige production of the year, it has been both an artistic and commercial disappointment, and it does not promise to match the domestic success of Solanas' *Tangos*).

Two of the three principal members of *Cine Liberación*, Gerardo Vallejo and Fernando Solanas, have returned to Argentina since the 1983 elections and have resumed film work there (the third, Octavio Getino, remains in Mexico). Vallejo has contributed another film to his ongoing project of developing a regional cinema in Tucumán, one of the most depressed regions in the Argentine interior. *El rigor del destino* (The Sternness of Fate, 1985), one of a very few Argentine films shot in the interior, is an emotional and nostalgic return to a rural social-folkloric theme. The release of Solanas' film this year, in contrast, heightened the debate over European versus Argentine styles. Set in Paris, begun in France while Solanas was in exile, winner of a Special Jury Award at the 1985 Venice Film Festival, *Tangos* has been criticized by some as being too "European" and "entertaining" for a Latin American political film. At the same time, a film such as *La historia oficial*, though thoroughly revisionist in its depiction of bourgeois anguish under the Junta*, has been praised for its ostensibly correct political line and the emotional power of its drama. This dichotomy, perpetuated mostly by foreign critics, seeks not only to relegate Latin American film production to the exclusively "political,"† but also misunderstands the historical context of progressive film-making in Argentina and skews the priorities of the reconstruc-

---

* The Junta was embraced with open arms by the national bourgeoisie in 1976 and for years refused to acknowledge its atrocities, benefitting at the same time from the Junta's *plata dulce* ("easy money") economic policies — noted only peripherally in *La historia oficial*.

† Solanas, for example, has lamented in recent interviews that no one interviews him about film art, only about politics.

La historia oficial *(The Official Story)*

tion of a critical national culture.

La historia oficial spearheaded, by virtue of its bland international style and thematic attention to the Argentine middle class, the Argentine film industry's reorientation towards the national middle class and the European and U.S. markets. (It is interesting to note that Puenzo came to film from a background in publicity, common enough in Argentine cinema but evident nonetheless in the film's style). *Tangos*, on the other hand, despite what some call a "European art-house" look, has to be considered one of the most distinctly Argentine films to be made since 1983. It will probably prove — it has only just been released at the time of this writing — second only to *La historia oficial* in domestic box-office receipts and international sales to date. It is also proving of greater interest to the more "popular" sectors of the Argentine and Latin American public.

In many respects, *Tangos* represents Solanas' return to the aborted project of 1973-75, the attempt to make entertaining mainstream films that combine social criticism with popular national culture. The lyrics of the tangos in the film were written by Solanas, who has a musical background, and the score was composed by the Argentine tango great Astor Piazzolla. But the film is also, according to Solanas, more than a tango musical; it is a *tanguedia* — part tango, part tragedy, part comedy, requisite ingredients of the national culture. The film is thus a clear homage to José Augustin Ferreyra, to his style and thematic concerns, and also of course to his own musical experimentation — *La muchacha de Arrabal* (1922), for which Ferreyra wrote lyrics to the film's live tango accompaniment. *Tangos*, however, presents a necessarily more radical view of Argentine popular culture: in Paris, the film's protagonists play tangos that have been banned by the military Junta that has forced them into exile.

It is hard to understand how an Argentine tango film, with cameo appearances from such historical personages as General San Martín and Carlos Gardel, could be regarded as more "European" than "Argentine" in style. Indeed, it is precisely in the context of a military Junta that banned certain tangos in its campaign to eliminate national culture that the political significance and cultural nationalism of the film should be clearly evident. The questions that this film should instead be raising concern the wisdom of a return to the golden age of the culture of the past, to tangos and to Ferreyra, in order to reconstruct a radical film culture in Argentina today.

Sectors of the non-Peronist Left have not failed to recognize the implicit cultural Peronism of *Tangos* — to recognize, in a word, its populism. As much as they disapprove of the internationalization of style by external market forces, they also reject a return to the "national-mythological" project that ended with the death of Perón over a decade ago. This approach, it is felt, might equally degenerate into a populist Latin American exoticism for the national working class and foreign markets alike.

An alternative approach can be seen in the work of Teo Kofman in his film *Perros de la noche* (Dogs in the Night, 1986, not yet released in Argentina or abroad at this writing). A gritty *lumpen* drama set in the shantytowns around Buenos Aires — a taboo topic — it is based on the caustic novel of the same name by Enrique Medina whose work, among other things, seeks to destroy the image of Buenos Aires as a cosmopolitan cultural capital, thus "Latin Americanizing" it. It is hard to tell, however, if this film, because of its fatalistic image of a social group too often ignored in Argentina, will find wide commercial success.

Nevertheless, it remains true that the Argentine cultural Left, like the political Left, must now "abandon the myths and phantasms of the past,"* (as one political commentator has put it), and rebuild a critical cinema, one that is responsive to the realities of contemporary Argentina. As I have mentioned, the death of populist politics has wide implications for the film industry, whose more progressive sectors have always followed a populist course. This does not mean, however, that the unique achievements and agenda of the 1973-75 period, the goal of widespread distribution and fidelity to popular national culture, should be abandoned.

Tangos: el exilio de Gardel

* Dabat, 1984.

The Roots of Documentary Realism
Fernando Birri

As founder of La Escuela Documental de Santa Fé, *the first
Latin American documentary film school, at the University of
Litoral, Argentina, Fernando Birri is recognized as a founder of
what was to become the New Latin American Cinema movement. Though political developments interrupted his work in
Latin America, even in his absence his example bore fruit in a
number of countries across the hemisphere. Birri has been living
in Rome since 1964, with frequent and prolonged visits to
Cuba, Mexico and Venezuela since 1979. In 1987 he will begin
work in Cuba with the film school there.*

*Julianne Burton interviewed Fernando Birri at the First
International Festival of the New Latin American Cinema, held
in Havana in December 1979. The interview was revised and
expanded at the second Havana festival, held the following year,
and was first published in Italian as "Fernando Birri: Pioniere e
Pellegrino" in Lino Miccichè, ed.,* Fernando Birri e la escuela
documental de Santa Fé, *17th Mostra Internazionale del Cinema
Nuovo, Pesaro, Italy, 1981. This slightly edited version omits
the section on his film* Los inundados *(The Flood Victims,
1961) and is reprinted from Julianne Burton's book* Cinema and
Social Change in Latin America: Conversations with Filmmakers *(University of Texas Press, Austin, 1986).*

Of Puppets and Poetry

In the beginning, I was a puppeteer. I'd had a puppet theater since I was a child. In the early forties, when I began my studies at the university, what had earlier been limited to my own household and neighborhood became a much more public activity. Somewhat in imitation of La Barraca, the traveling theater group founded in Pre-Civil War Spain by Federico García Lorca, a group of us would take that puppet theater on tour — to schools, orphanages, insane asylums, jails — around the city of Santa Fé and the province of El Litoral.

Later I moved on from puppets to flesh-and-blood actors, directing the first university theater group at the *Universidad Nacional del Litoral*. My goal as director remained the same: to reach the broadest possible audience within the popular sector. This concern explains, in part, why I was to turn eventually to filmmaking.

My deepest creative roots, however, are in poetry. I began writing poetry as a child, and continue to do so; it is the foundation of all my work. As a puppeteer, as a theater director, as a filmmaker — what has guided my steps is nothing other than the search for and expression of a poetics.

I come from a generation that was practically born with the movies. From early childhood, I went to the movies almost daily. I remember seeing Al Jolson's *The Jazz Singer* while sitting on my father's lap. When, at the height of my success as a theater director, I opted for filmmaking as a career, it was because I realized that neither poetry nor theatre could offer me access to audiences larger than those I was already reaching.

The Roots of Political Awareness

Logically enough, this eagerness to reach the broadest possible audience, which characterizes all my work, has a lot to do with my own background and class consciousness. My popular roots are still fresh. I'm a typical Argentine because I am the second generation of an immigrant family. Hard times and intrusive *carabinieri* prompted my anarchist grandfather, a farmer and miller from northern Italy, to emigrate to Argentina around 1880. Many years later, similar circumstances would force me to make the same journey, but in reverse.

Once in Argentina, my grandparents moved from the rural to the urban proletariat. My father "moved up in the world" one step more, earning his doctoral degree in social and political sciences at the *Universidad Nacional del Litoral*. Despite his rise in status, however, he never abandoned his father's political convictions.

I read Georgi Plekhanov's *Art and Society* in my father's library at the age of eleven. From a relatively tender age, I was aware of the social class I belonged to, and in the act of becoming class conscious, I also became conscious of my own determination to dedicate all my energies to opposing the value system of my class, the ascendant petite bourgeoisie.

It would have been more gratifying to identify myself with the peasantry or the working class, but it would have also been a falsification and a grave ideological error, leading me to seek my reflection in a mirror that held another image. It was only through the process of recognizing my own bourgeois roots that I could marshal all my intellectual arms to undermine the bourgeois values within my personality and transform them into the values of the popular classes.

But this is not a purely intellectual process; there's an emotional component as well. On a gut level, I have always been on the side of the underdogs, the injured and degraded, the wretched of the earth. As soon as I disowned my bourgeois privilege and took on the responsibilities of an intellectual who belongs to a revolutionary class, I become a part of the injured and degraded. So my class position was a conscious choice.

To Learn to Make Movies

Along with Mexico and Brazil, Argentina has traditionally been one of the great film centers in Latin America. During the early fifties, when I decided to become a filmmaker, the regime of Gen. Juan Perón had diminished and debased the national film industry.* Despite this, I decided to leave my native Santa Fé and journey to Buenos Aires to learn to make movies.

* Whether or not Perón debased the Argentine film industry is a subject of great debate. But he certainly didn't diminish it; see the annual production figures from 1943-1958 in the chronology in this volume. [ed.]

I began looking for work as an assistant producer, but I soon learned to lower my sights until, finally, I offered myself to *Argentina Sono Film* as a janitor. Nothing doing. It seems that all jobs in the film industry were controlled by a kind of mafia. For the likes of me, all doors were closed.

I decided that I would learn filmmaking wherever it was taught and found out about the two leading European film schools — *IDHEC* in Paris and the *Centro Sperimentale di Cinematografia* in Rome.

Like film fans anywhere in that period, I was most informed about (and most "deformed" by) Hollywood films. I had seen only a limited number of European films — French, Swedish, German — at the film society we had founded in Sante Fé. But at the time I was deciding on a career, postwar Italian Neorealism was taking movie houses around the world by storm. *Bicycle Thief, Rome, Open City,* and *La terra trema* had all appeared in the late forties. For me, the great revelation of the Neorealist movement was that, contrary to Hollywood's tenets and example, it was possible to make movies on the same artistic level as a play, a novel, or a poem.

I enrolled in the *Centro Sperimentale* because it enabled me to be at the center of that important film movement and because it provided practical as well as theoretical training. While studying for my degree, I made several documentaries, worked as assistant to Zavattini and DeSica on *Il tetto*, and acted in Francesco Maselli's first film. I tried to study the film-making process from every angle, to master it as a totality.

The Return to Argentina

In 1955 Perón was overthrown, to be replaced by the famous "Liberating Revolution," which would find its most effective leader in Gen. Pedro Aramburu. In 1956 I decided to return to Argentina to pursue my life and work on my own soil. The prospect of having to leave again was unthinkable.

Cartoonists have always depicted Argentina as a dwarf with a giant's head: the oversized head is the capital, Buenos Aires, and the tiny body symbolizes the rest of the country. Film production had always been located in the giant's head. It was clear to me from the first that I was going to have trouble striking any bargains there to do what I thought was necessary to create a new Argentine cinema.

So I decided to give up on Buenos Aires and return to my native Santa Fé, prepared to see if there, starting from zero, I could begin to produce a kind of filmmaking that had nothing to do with the mercantile-industrial setup in the capital. What I wanted was to discover the face of an invisible Argentina — invisible not because it couldn't be seen, but because no one *wanted* to see it.

In Santa Fé, I returned once again to the *Universidad Nacional del Litoral,* where I had studied law, since, in Argentina as in so many other Latin American countries, the university is a kind of "free zone" that offers its shelter to a lot of "unconventional" activities. The Institute of Sociology asked me to organize a four-day seminar on filmmaking. The fervid enthusiasm of the dozens of young people who attended ensured that the seminar was only a beginning.

Photodocumentaries

After briefly situating the problem in theoretical terms, I immediately confronted my students with a practical task: making photodocumentaries. The idea was simply to venture forth with a still camera and any available tape recorder in search of one's own environment — to converse with and photograph people, places, animals, plants, but mainly *problems* of one's surroundings. One hundred and twenty eager photographers scattered themselves around the city and its outskirts in search of potential topics for a future national cinema.

The experiment produced a rich harvest of themes, all of them informed by an explicit social awareness and concern. *Tire dié,* about the children begging along the railroad trestles, would provide the basis for the first filmed social survey *(encuestra social)* in Latin America. Others included *El conventillo,* on overcrowded housing; *Nuncia,* about a street vendor; *Mercado de abasto* (The Meat Market); *Un boliche* (A Tavern); and *A la cola* (Get in Line), about the consequences of the lack of modern sanitation facilities.

As a result of this seminar, the Institute of Sociology decided to establish an Institute of Cinematography, which would, eventually, assume independence and its own name: *La Escuela Documental de Santa Fé* (The Documentary School of Santa Fé).

Theory and Practice

My work has always been shaped by a refusal to separate theory from practice. Each film I've made — from *Tire dié*, where I had 120 assistants, through *Los inundados*, where I had nearly 80, to my most recent film, *Org*, where I had only one — has been a film/school. I do not believe in "formal" education; I believe in learning by doing. Theory and practice must go hand in hand. I would say — without bias and without hesitation — that practice has to be the key, with theory as its guide and interpreter. This is the foundation on which the first school of documentary filmmaking in Latin America was built.

I returned from Europe with the idea of founding a film school modeled after the *Centro Sperimentale*, where directors, actors, cinematographers, scenographers, sound technicians, and so on, would receive all their training — in short, a school that would produce *fiction* filmmakers. Back in Santa Fé, once I saw the actual conditions of the city and the country I realized that such a school would be premature. What was needed was a school that would combine the basics of filmmaking with the basics of sociology, history, geography, and politics. Because the real undertaking at hand was a quest for national identity, an identity that had been lost or alienated by a system of economic and political as well as cultural hegemony established by the dominant classes in concert first with Spanish colonizers, later with British investors, and most recently with agents of the United States.

This need to seek out a national identity was what prompted me to pose the problem in strictly *documentary* terms. It is my belief that the first step to be taken by an aspiring national film industry is to document national reality. And so the *Escuela Documental* concentrated on developing the three major types of cineastes necessary to the documentary: directors, cinematographers, and producers. The organization of the school evolved day by day, on a hit-or-miss basis, guided by our ongoing self-criticism.

Tire dié: Genesis of the First Filmed Social Survey

An exhibition of the original photodocumentaries toured not only the Santa Fé region and Buenos Aires, but other parts of the country as well, ranging as far as Montevideo, at the invitation of the organizers of the *SODRE* film festival.* Our first film project was an outgrowth of that initial experiment with photodocumentaries. From among them we chose the one that seemed to have the most rigor and the greatest impact, the one that offered the fullest opportunity for denouncing a deplorable set of social conditions.

After two years' work and innumerable obstacles, *Tire dié* was transformed from a photodocumentary into a film. We had very few resources. We shot with two borrowed cameras and film stock that was either donated or wangled out of the university. Our tape recorder was not exactly up to professional standards. I remember how we would go every afternoon to those often-flooded lowlands where the film was shot, carrying our modest cameras and the tape recorder's giant battery in a strongbox. The weight of those batteries would sink us up to our knees in mud.

The premiere of *Tire dié* in the Great Hall of the *Universidad Nacional del Litoral* was an event unparalleled in the annals of Argentine university history. The auditorium was filled to capacity with people from the most varied social backgrounds — from august university professors to the little street kids who appear in the film, all dressed up in their cleanest shirt, but barefoot as always, since they had no shoes. We had to screen the film three times. At one o'clock in the morning it was still rolling.

That first version was about an hour long. We showed it to everyone who appeared in it, taking it around the slums of Santa Fé and discussing it with people. Film students made up hundreds of questionnaires inquiring about which parts were

* Sponsored by Uruguay's Radio-Electric Broadcasting Society (SODRE) from the early fifties through the late sixties (with a hiatus from 1962 to 1965), this short-film festival gave impetus and visibility to the incipient movement of politically committed documentaries, particularly in the Southern Cone. [J.B.]

effective, which were not, and why. All these data were compiled before cutting the definitive, thirty-three-minute version.

Given the poor quality of our tape recorder, the original soundtrack was virtually unintelligible. But because it was a survey film, it was essential that the audience be able to understand what the interviewees said. So when we made the final cut, we had to do something with the soundtrack as well. We laid on an additional soundtrack in which a leading Argentine actor and actress repeat the key information, serving as intermediaries between the subjects of the film and the audience.

Inspired by my then-remote experiences with the traveling puppet theater, we continued to distribute *Tire dié* and our subsequent films with a primitive "mobile cinema," which consisted of a truck and a projector. Years later, when I made my first trip to Cuba, the first thing I asked to see was a mobile cinema unit. I was taken to the Zapata Swamp to see the screening of a Charlie Chaplin film. It was enormously moving and gratifying to see that what we had attempted with such modest means was being implemented with all the resources a new socialist state could offer.

After *Tire dié*, we made numerous other documentaries, among them *La innundación de Santa Fé* (The Flooding of Santa Fé), *El palanquero* (The Pile Driver), *El puente de papel* (The Paper Bridge), and *Los 40 cuartos* (The Forty Rooms). The photodocumentary and the interviews continued to serve as a first step to the filmed documentary.

The End of an Experiment

A handful of other films were the product of a different approach. *La pampa gringa*, a historical film whose purpose was to commemorate the role played by European immigrants in opening up the Argentine *pampa*, was constructed from old family photographs. The word *gringo* in this context refers to Europeans of many nationalities, but principally to the Italians. The film reconstructs the history of the town called Esperanza (hope) — telling name — a colony founded near Santa Fé in the mid-nineteenth century. *La primera fundación de Buenos Aires* (The First Founding of Buenos Aires, 1959) was another composite film, based not on photographs but on the cartoon drawings of a popular humorist, Oski.

Commercial distribution of documentary shorts was problematic at best. The new film legislation passed after Perón's ouster decreed that every feature-length film in commercial release had to be accompanied by a short, but in fact the law was not consistently enforced. To overcome this problem, I hit on a solution that was later to be used in several other Latin American countries as well: I strung several thematically related shorts together and distributed them as a feature-length film. *Che, Buenos Aires* combined two documentary shorts of mine with two by other filmmakers; all four had the capital city as their theme.

These compilation documentaries were "innocent" enough, but the work of the *Escuela Documental* on contemporary themes was beginning to draw official disapproval and, eventually, censure. From an official standpoint, the definitive proof of the school's subversive nature was the film called *Los 40 cuartos* (1962), our second filmed survey, about conditions in an overcrowded tenement called *El conventillo*. After being shown as part of the Annual Short Film Showcase organized by the National Board of Culture, the film was confiscated and banned. No amount of public pressure succeeded in obtaining either the film's release or an explanation.

This and other serious problems made it clear to me that I would not long be able to continue as director of the school, which was being labeled a "center for subversive activities." Let's be frank: in fact, it *was*. What kind of subversion? Artistic subversion because we questioned *everything*; political and professional subversion because we were training people different from those who controlled the rest of the Argentine film industry. Our subjects, our goals, our methodology — everything was different.

My last act as director of the *Escuela Documental* was to assemble a documentary history of our experience from 1956 to 1963. For anyone who has lived through such tumultuous years, ardently involved in political struggle, it would have been all too easy and all too human to subjectivize and thus distort one's account. To avoid this danger, I decided to limit myself to compiling the most relevant materials produced over that seven year period and publishing them in book form.* I was careful to document all the films we made and all the people who worked on them. Many people whose names appear there — Gerardo Vallejo, Diego Bonacina, Jorge Goldenberg, Manuel Horacio Giménez, for example — subsequently spread their filmmaking skills over the length and breadth of Latin America. Others, like Raymundo Gleyzer and Jorge Cedrón, don't appear at all because, during my tenure at least, their ties to the school were more indirect.

The Roads of Exile

With the fall of the Frondizi government and the installation of a military regime, I knew I had to leave. But I did not go alone. Five of us left together as a kind of "scouting party" to investigate what was going on elsewhere in Latin America and, eventually, to create alternative possibilities for those who had stayed behind. In late 1963 we crossed the northern border in semiclandestine fashion. To have left through Buenos Aires would have meant leaving our films behind.

For what seemed like endless days and nights we traveled in an infernal little train across the Brazilian state of Rio Grande do Sul before finally arriving at São Paulo, where we had a number of contacts, among them two former students — Vlado Herzog and Maurice Capovilla.[†] Those filmmakers introduced us to others, including future director Sérgio Muniz and future producer Thomaz Farkas, historian and critic Paulo Emílio Salles Gomes, and Rudá Andrade, director of the Cinémathèque at the Museum of Modern Art in São Paulo.

Andrade organized a retrospective of our work at the museum, which led to other invitations for lectures and screenings and, eventually, to a plan for a series of documentaries. We began with four short films. Instead of planning them in the conventional way, to be produced one after the other, we decided to

---

* Fernando Birri, *La Escuela Documental de Santa Fé* (Santa Fé, Argentina: Editorial Documento del Instituto de Cinematografia de la Universidad Nacional del Litoral, 1964). [J.B.]

† Vladimir Herzog, filmmaker and prominent television journalist in São Paulo, was arrested in 1975 and died in detention shortly thereafter. His death sparked a massive wave of protest around the country. Maurice Capovilla continues to work in film and television in Brazil [J.B.]

produce them all simultaneously. This would not have been possible without the generous financial backing provided by Thomaz Farkas and the unsurpassed production skills of one of the *Escuela Documental's* most outstanding students, Edgardo Pallero, who had left Argentina with me. The four documentaries — Gerard Sarno's *Viramundo*, Paulo Gil Soares's *Memória do cangaço* (Memory of the Cangaço), Manuel Horacio Giménez's *Nossa escola do samba* (Our Samba School), and Maurice Capovilla's *Subterrâneos do futebol* (Soccer Underground) — are now landmarks in Brazilian film history, the first examples of an unparalleled series of documentaries on Brazilian culture produced by Thomaz Farkas over a period of several years.

Our experience with the group in São Paulo led to contacts with filmmakers in Rio de Janeiro and then to my own plans for a feature film based on a book on Brazilian popular culture, *Jõao Boa Morte* by Ferreira Gullar.

The political situation in Brazil at this time (early 1964) was very volatile. Jõao Goulart, a progressive, was president. Many sectors of the population were mobilized, among them the peasantry. I remember standing in a public square with some fellow filmmakers while endless truckloads of machete-bearing *campesinos* arrived to hear Goulart decree Brazil's first land reform.

A short time later, as in Argentina under Frondizi, the colonels decided to let Goulart's head roll.* With the military coup of 1 April 1964, I stood by powerless for the second time while my prospects of pursuing the kind of filmmaking to which I was committed were shut down in my face. As a militant who has struggled his whole life long to avoid the separation of personal history and public history, I have had to pay the high price of subordinating my work and my opportunities as a filmmaker to historical circumstances.

Although the Brazilian situation still held some possibilities for my friends and collaborators, it was clear that the kind of feature-length films I had hoped to make there had become impossible. We all agreed that I had to detach myself from our

---

* This expression is purely metaphorical, since the ousted Goulart fled to the safety of his Uruguayan ranch rather than confront the military. [J.B.]

little group and go off to see what alternatives existed in other Latin American territories.

I traveled to Mexico, where I spoke with Emilio García Riera, leading film historian and critic, and with Gabriel García Márquez, who was at that time a frustrated screenwriter in Mexico. Despite sporadic attempts at a "new Mexican cinema," the situation there was quite bleak.

In mid-1964, I arrived in Cuba, where I was greeted with great affection and solidarity. But there, too, the situation was difficult. Cuban filmmakers had to confront grave problems, including severe shortages of equipment and foreign exchange. After some disastrous experiments in coproduction with other countries, it was clear that the first priority was consolidating the internal organization of the Cuban Film Institute. It was not the moment for me to propose another kind of collaboration.

It was only after this long pilgrimage in search of filmmaking opportunities within Latin America, having left no possible stone unturned, that I decided to return to Italy. It was neither a wished for nor a voluntary decision, but one reached out of desperation. I returned to the place where I had been trained and had practiced as a filmmaker in the belief that it might offer opportunities to pursue work that I could not undertake in Latin America at that particular time.

We militant filmmakers are dependent on the "permissiveness", however limited, of bourgeois democratic governments. When the dark night of fascism constricts the room for maneuver offered by more "liberal" regimes, which have a stake, at least, in keeping up appearances, we all face the same range of options: to try to pursue our work in our own country, despite the heightened repression; to "lie low" and wait until circumstances improve; to emigrate to another country in Latin America; or to abandon the continent. Any one of these options might be valid, depending on the particular circumstances, and they must be taken into account when judging the work of any filmmaker.

From Nationalistic to Cosmic, from Realistic to Raving, from Popular to Lumpen

My experience as a filmmaker begins with a manifesto entitled "For a Nationalist, Realist, Critical and Popular Cinema" and culminates in another manifesto, entitled "For a Cosmic Cinema, Raving and Lumpen." The breadth of the trajectory is a product of expansion rather than of negation.

This latest manifesto, a poem published in conjunction with the screening at the Venice film festival of my latest film, *Org*, is proof of the fact that I am more than ever a "foreign element" in the country where I have lived now for fifteen years. Consistent with one of the attitudes that has shaped my entire life and work, my years in Italy have been marked by the conscious decision *not* to become a part of Italian life. However painful it may be, I cannot disguise my own condition; I cannot cease to be an uprooted Latin American trying to build a life in exile. Naturally, I take part in the life around me — I attend demonstrations, I participate in debates — but always with the awareness that I am a "marginal" being in the Italian context, and that my "marginalization" has been a conscious choice.

The film I have just completed, *Org*, is also a "marginal" film. Slowly, like a snail that leaves behind a silvery trail, I've assembled the film as I've gone about living my daily life, until the two have become indistinguishable to me. The film is a poem, a fantasy, a Rorschach test for the spectator, more visceral than rational, aimed less at the conscious mind than at the subconscious.

Although it grows out of my filmmaking experiences in Latin America, I don't believe that *Org* belongs with what I call my "Latin American cycle"; but, if pressed, I have to concede that in a sense the film participates in and even anticipates the difficulties and contradictions that countless Latin American filmmakers have been compelled to face, given the tragic historical events that have plagued Latin American political life since the Bolivian coup of 1971 and the overthrow of the Popular Unity government in Chile in 1973.

Evaluation of an Experience

I occasionally hear about other filmmakers who, years later and in relatively distant countries, have developed an approach similar to the one we evolved at the *Escuela Documental de Santa Fé*. A relatively recent example would be the work of the Colombian documentarists Marta Rodríguez and Jorge Silva. If our experiences parallel each other, the links need not be direct ones. I believe that, on the one hand, the need to confront one's national reality and, on the other, the scarcity of resources endemic to politically committed filmmaking in Latin America, mean that basically unrelated experiences converge in necessity. Our efforts in Santa Fé grew out of a real and vital necessity. Ours was a pilot experience that later took wings throughout the continent, not because of the creative impulse of a single individual but because of the needs and imperatives of a social, political, and historical reality that was bound to find many spokespeople.

There are basically two kinds of filmmakers: one invents an imaginary reality; the other confronts an existing reality and attempts to understand it, analyze it, criticize it, judge it, and, finally, translate it into film. In the latter case, the lasting validity of the work can only be corroborated in space and time, that is, by history and geography. The New Latin American Cinema movement, as it has evolved and spread over the length and breadth of Latin America during the past twenty years, has somehow justified those of us who decided so many years ago to seek out our own national reality and try to communicate it. Not to invent it, but to *re-invent* it: to interpret and transform it.

This First International Festival of New Latin American Cinema here in Havana has given us the opportunity to survey and evaluate the work of the past decade. We stand now on a summit from which we can also make out some of the contours that lie ahead. I believe that the time is ripe for renewal, because the only true revolution is a permanent revolution.

Translated by Julianne Burton

Tire dié (Throw Me a Dime), *1958*

For a Nationalist, Realist, Critical and Popular Cinema

Fernando Birri

The New Latin American Cinema, which we continue to call "new" in order to exorcise any possible regression, is now about 25 years old. It was born in Cuba with *El megano* by García Espinosa, Gutiérrez Alea, Alfredo Guevara and José Massip; in Brazil with Nelson Pereira dos Santos; and in Argentina with the Documentary Film School of Santa Fé. Something I always like to remember is that it was born without any kind of, let's say, confabulation between us, but because it was in the air. We can now understand it with great clarity, thanks to something the Italians call *il senno di poi*, that is, the sign that comes afterwards, seeing history through the other end of the telescope. It was born because in that moment, in the middle of the '50s, in different places in Latin America, a generation of filmmakers was growing up who wanted to provide a reply to some of the problems of the moment, and who brought with them more questions than answers. They were questions that came from an historical necessity, a necessity in the history of our peoples; in the history of people awakening with great strength to the consciousness of occupying their place in history, a place denied us for so many years, a place which, once and for all, as the title of the beautiful Nicaraguan film has it, is a place of bread and dignity. These two ideas, I believe, explain something of the tension out of which the New Latin American Cinema was created and motivated.

When we were born, nothing was clear and resolved; we had no recipes of prefabricated formulae. What we did know was that in some ways this continent was so rich, so complex, so contradictory, so coarse, so exaltant in other ways, that it was a continent that was not reflected in the images produced by the three major Latin American cinemas, the only ones that existed: the Mexican, the Brazilian and the Argentine cinemas.

This new cinema was born with two or three keys to comprehension, analysis, interpretation and expression. What were they? I remember that when *Tire dié* came out in 1958, it was accompanied by a short manifesto arguing for a national, realist and critical cinema. These were the three keys which in one way or another tried theoretically to illustrate a concrete formulation, the film that was *Tire dié*. From *Tire dié* we passed to *Los inundados*, which is already a fictional film though with a documentary base — and this is another constant in the new Latin American cinema, that is, the documentary support. A characteristic that has been progressively accentuated is the rupture with traditional genres: with what is traditionally understood by documentary; with what is traditionally understood or understandable as narrative.

Nelson Pereira dos Santos had always worked in narrative cinema. But apart from being the first attempt of this kind at Santa Fé, *Los inundados* was an attempt to achieve a greater diffusion of the film object, to explore the possibility of more extensive communication by the film with its public. And in that sense, the narrative construction has a much greater power of communication, and can embrace a much wider horizon than the documentary. Narrative cinema adds to the three previous keys the new key of the popular. In this way, the theoretical postulate which accompanied our work was the call for a nationalist, realist and critical cinema, but, additionally, it was intrinsically related to a fourth, the popular, which is to say, it tried to interpret, express and communicate with the people.

This is also related to another tendency which the New Latin American Cinema has always had, which is its aspiration to be an active cinema. What does this mean? It means that in the last instance it is a cinema which is generated within the reality, it becomes concrete on a screen and from this screen returns to reality, aspiring to transform it. This is the fundamental idea. Over the years I have often asked myself what could be a common denominator for the New Latin American Cinema. If I had to give a brief definition, I would say that it's a cinema which corresponds to what I called and continued to call a poetics of the transformation of reality. That's to say, that it generates a creative energy which throughout cinema aspires to modify the reality upon which it is projected. We applied this concept to documentary as much as narrative, to short as well as medium and long films, and now we're applying it also to television, to which we are now equally dedicating our forces. In this concept of a poetics of the transformation of reality it is necessary, among other things, to have no abyss between life and the screen.

Federico García Lorca once introduced Pablo Neruda very beautifully at the University of Madrid, many years ago, before 1936, when Pablo wasn't yet fully Pablo. I remember that Federico said that Pablo was a poet — and he would have wanted to say this of our cinema — closer to blood than to ink, closer to death than philosophy, and who carried in his blood — and I would say this is true of our celluloid — that grain of madness without which it's not worth living. In short, the cinema that started to be made 25 years ago was a utopia, and now this cinema exists and has a continental dimension. This is an important datum. It is the only cinema in the history of cinema that expresses a continent in all the diversity of its cultural-historical connotations but which, at the same time, belongs to an economic infrastructure which perpetuates its so-called underdevelopment, and which places us face to face with common and shared problems of existence.

In this sense, then, it seems to me that the characterisations we're trying to develop of an active cinema for an active spectator — a spectator who doesn't consume passively as if merely digesting celluloid — also has another aspect: that it's a cinema of and for liberation, for economic, political and cultural liberation, and also the liberation of the image, which is to say, of imagination. This also seems to me a characteristic of the New Latin American Cinema, present in its origins and course of development, deepening and clarifying with daily practice. And we feel this liberation of the image to be valid in the face of the successive crises through which the New Latin American Cinema has passed. It was reflected in the Havana Film Festival in 1981, when we conducted a seminar on cinema and poetic imagination. This cinema, though it has to do above all with reality and has to intervene in the real in order to transform it, cannot do without the word poetic and the creative energy which the word contains. It is intrinsic in the need to expand our horizons. It is like the tension of an arrow in flight towards a target it has not yet reached. That is the new poetic-political cinema which is being produced in Latin America; and another indication of the crisis that is manifest in this Fifth Havana Festival (1984). Crisis is a word which manifestly some people don't at all like because it means above all change. Certainly, if the change is towards old age, senility, arteriosclerosis, one can understand ... if the change is from life to death, obviously this crisis is fatal. But if the crisis is the first cry of the baby at its birth, or the rupture or laceration of an adolescent who is beginning to pose the big questions which perhaps have no answer, the big insoluble questions, then it's very positive because it's a crisis of growth and a crisis of maturation.

Translated by Michael Chanan

For a Cosmic Cinema, Raving and Lumpen: The First Cosmunist (Cosmic Communist) Manifesto
Fernando Birri

. . . tick thinking guts:
cosmunism cosmic and magical communism
for a cosmic cinema, raving and lumpen
totally disputable because of its methods
and shooting and editing time
(but the whole operation is a
demonstration that Utopia can
be put into practice) madness and rigor
hand-in-hand there will be no lasting revolution

without the revolution of language
tabula rasa: cinema from zero to
experiment ORG as a non-film
an experience with each
individual spectator ("only for
crazy people") totally disputable because of its
methods and shooting and editing time
the verification of a cinema for mutants
a total cinema ORGexperience as
experiment: hope of communication
(Pythagorean, oracular, alquimistic
montage techniques) "montage of attractions"
new mental-ludic dimension (but the whole
operation is a demonstration that
Utopia can be put into practice)
(the public not as a "mass" but as a re-uniting
of individual spectators) madness and rigor
hand-in-hand (between cinema and non-cinema or
beyond-cinema: filmunculus) (a filmic Rorschach
test) thereby ideologizing everything
but also sensorializing everything heir to
the travelling magic lantern carriers
in order to experience oneself in answer
to the stimulus ORG there will be no lasting revolution
without revolutionizing language
sensual hedonistic erotic communism
thinking guts: cosmunism
fabrication of a poem or a
novel the clash of artisanship and industry
cosmic and magical communism for a
cosmic cinema, raving and lumpen . . .

Translated by Julianne Burton

Argentina: A Huge Case of Censorship
Alfonso Gumucio Dagron

The following account of film censorship in Argentina is excerpted from the definitive history of film censorship in Latin America, Cine, censura y exilio en América Latina *(1979), by Bolivian filmmaker and critic Alfonso Gumucio Dagron. Written in the late 1970s, at the height of the repression of the military Junta that seized power in 1976, this article does not foresee the fall of that Junta following its military defeat to Britain in 1982 in the Malvinas Islands dispute. Since the election of Raúl Alfonsín in 1983, censorship has been abolished by an act of Congress and the film censorship board has once again returned to the task of classifying films by age.*

"In Argentina, we're totally boxed in by censorship," Fernando Solanas declared during an interview in June 1968, shortly before the world premiere of one of the most talked about Latin American films, *La hora de los hornos* (The Hour of the Furnaces), at the *IV Mostra Internazionale del Cinema Nuovo* in Pesaro, Italy. Solanas knew what he was talking about. His work as an activist filmmaker with Octavio Getino and other members of the *Cine Liberación* group was always surrounded by censorship. That censorship became more extreme as the years went by and peaked in 1976 under the dictatorship of General Videla with the exile of many Argentine filmmakers, and the persecution, incarceration, and death of others.

As in most countries in South America, film censorship has always been practised in Argentina, with or without a law that defined the limit of what was allowed. The first censorship legislation dates from 1957, but it is evident that the censors' activities predate it, at least as far as foreign films are concerned. In fact, national film production, until the end of the 1950s, did not really warrant the attention of the censors. Films such as *Las aguas bajan turbias* (Troubled Waters, 1952), by Hugo del Carril, about the slavery of workers on *yerba mate* plantations, did not really go so far as to expose actual working conditions. Other filmmakers such as Leopoldo Torre Nilsson and Fernando Ayala fitted even more snugly in the film industry of the day, always one of the most important on the continent, with those of Brazil and Mexico.

During the presidency of Perón, these filmmakers were carried along by an inertia made possible by the Law of Compulsory Exhibition of Argentine film, which assured them a market for their films. Lucas Demare, who made *La guerra gaucha* in 1942, ended his career making such mediocre films as *Los isleros* (The Islanders, 1951) and *Mercado de abasto* (The Meat Market, 1954). Luis Saslavsky left the country in 1948, during Perón's reign, and continued his career in Spain, after making *Historia de una mala mujer* (The Story of an Unfaithful Woman), his last Argentine film before returning to the country after the fall of Perón.

With the fall of Perón in 1955, Ernesto Arancibia, León Klimovsky, Hugo Fregonese, Enrique Cahen Salaberry, Tulio Demichelli, Vignoly Barreto and others became political exiles from the new military regime. Except for Hugo Fregonese, who went to work in Hollywood, all of them headed for Spain, where they have resided since. Under Frondizi, who was elected in 1958, the necessary conditions for making films were not present, although Torre Nilsson was prolific at *Argentina Sono Film*. Simply put, the entire film industry began to roll in slow motion. From fifty or more films per year in the early 1950s, production dropped to thirty-six features in 1956 and fifteen in 1957. With the arrival of Frondizi, more than thirty films were made, and in the coming years production stabilized around this figure.

At the beginning of the 1960s, a supposed "New Argentine Cinema" was promoted. It was, in fact, nothing of the kind. A new generation was coming into the industry, but they brought with them the same old ideas and fears as always. Frondizi's censorship sent these directors on a search whose paths were not at all original, as they were shamelessly inspired by the European New Wave. These directors discovered Ingmar Bergman, Michelangelo Antonioni, and the young French directors, and attempted to transpose their style onto a cosmopolitan Buenos Aires. They adapted the novels and short stories of Julio Cortázar and other Argentine writers, but they could not overcome the limitations of the industry that had come to consider itself as producing a cinema for intellectuals. We should not confuse these directors with those who built, on the margins of the industry, a true cinema of national expression.

The real national cinema, the cinema that by openly showing the Argentine reality would provoke the reaction of the censors, had been developing since 1956 at the *Escuela Documental de Santa Fé* (Documentary Film School) at the University of Litoral, led by Fernando Birri. Birri came out of the Italian neo-realist movement, and had experienced it first hand while studying at the *Centro Sperimentale di Cinematografia* in Rome, with such masters as Luigi Chiarini and Cesare Zavattini. When transplanted to Argentina, this neo-realism did not become just another fad, another trend among many, but a useful tool to turn people's eyes towards reality. For the first time, people witnessed the country's social reality and, as a result, Birri's films *Tire dié* (Throw Me a Dime, 1958) and *Los inundados* (The Flood Victims, 1961) met head on with the censors. This was even more the case when these films began to collect prizes and attract attention in Europe. They are films which show to the world an image of Argentina that the ruling class would like very much to hide, insofar as they allude to that class' responsibility — or irresponsibility.

These subversive films, however, could not be more elementary, simple, or innocent. *Tire dié* is a documentary on the misery of a slum through which a train runs every day. Poor, barefoot children trot along beside it, begging the travellers looking out the window to throw them a dime. "Throw me a dime, throw me a dime," they plead, looking up with their dirty, anguished faces. For the first time in Latin America, interviews with residents of a shantytown were included in a film.

Birri also included interviews in *Los inundados*, which was viciously attacked by the censors, perhaps because it was a feature length film. A flood, a natural disaster, provided Birri with an excuse to undertake a social analysis of the country's alienated people, of the exploited. The film, inspired by a story by Mateo Booz, but structured as a social survey, closely followed the case of one family affected by the flood.

The police reacted by proscribing the film, and tried to seize all copies in circulation. The censor was offended when the film won prizes at the European festivals of Venice and Karlovy Vary in 1962. How could a film that showed only squalor, that mocked the authorities, and, to top it off, was "badly done", win an award? Birri, in defending the film, said that the technical imperfections were the result of the non-professional means he had been forced to work with, and that he preferred "the contents to the technique, to make sense imperfectly than to have a senseless perfection."

The Argentine authorities did all they could to halt screenings of *Los inundados.* In 1961, the *Instituto Nacional de Cinematografía* refused five times in a row to grant either an A or a B classification to the film, so that it could benefit from the institute's export and mandatory exhibition provisions. After these five failed attempts, the film was finally granted an A classification, though not without difficulty — it obtained the bare minimum number of votes required, against the opposition of the Buenos Aires exhibitors.* The matter did not end there. In April 1962, the jury of the film institute granted cash prizes to fifteen Argentine films, and they preferred to award one million *pesos* to the film *La burrerita de Ipacarai* (The Donkey Girl from Ipacarai), a pornographic film with Isabel Sarli, by Armando Bo, rather than award *Los inundados* any prize at all. The film, meanwhile, was attracting attention in other countries. It was invited to screen at Cannes, but the film institute sent *Setente veces siete* (Seventy Times Seven, by Leopoldo Torre Nilsson) instead. In May of that year an invitation from the Locarno Film Festival was never officially acknowledged. When the film finally made it to the festivals of Karlovy Vary and Venice, during August and September of that year, it was awarded the prize of Best Opera Prima (first film) at the latter, a distinction that until that time no other Argentine film had

---

* The exhibitors were then obliged to show the film in their theatres under the mandatory exhibition law. [ed.]

ever received at a foreign film festival.

One of the darkest periods of Argentine film censorship began in 1963, when the lawyer Ramiro de la Fuente took over the administration of the censor board. De la Fuente was an ultra-conservative Catholic who reigned unchallenged for ten years. It would be a never-ending task to list all the films he cut or banned during that period. When Frederick Rossif's documentary *To Die in Madrid* was screened, de la Fuente himself showed up at the cinema and, according to the magazine *Visión*, "left carrying the reels of film on his very own anti-Republican shoulders," to paraphrase Carlos Alvarez. The previous year the board, led by this same man, had police seize copies of *La herencia* (The Inheritance), an Argentine film by Ricardo Alventosa.

In 1963, the law 8.205/63 authorized the beginning of the most severe period of censorship known until then in Argentina. De la Fuente did not hesitate to make full use of the decree, and he banned or butchered such films as Bergman's *The Silence*, and Buñuel's *Viridiana*, as well as such national films as *Los jovenes viejos* (The Old Youngsters) by Rodolfo Kuhn, Mario Soffici's *Barrio gris* (Grey Neighbourhood), Lautaro Murúa's *Alias Gardelito* and David Kohon's *Tres veces Ana* (Three Times Ana).

The influence of ultra-Catholics on the board becomes visible when one checks its composition in 1966. Aside from the three members from the Ministry of Defense and the representative from the Ministry of the Interior, there appears a representative of the Parents' League, a representative of the Mothers' League (a curious separation, by the way), a representative of the Family Institute, another from the Christian Family Movement (up to this point it's "all in the family"), one from the Institute for the Protection of Young Women, another from the International Union for the Protection of Children, and finally, a representative of the Private Union for Assistance to Minors. On the whole, a tribunal worthy of the most Holy Inquisition. De la Fuente was in fact known by the filmmakers as the "Argentine Torquemada."*

* Tomás de Torquemada was a Spanish Inquisitor responsible for the expulsion of the Jews from Spain in 1492 and noted for his unusually harsh sentences. [ed.]

The censors really began to show their political face by the end of the 1960s, when films began to appear that referred to the national reality in equally political terms. The most notorious example is no doubt *La hora de los hornos*. Fernando Solanas and Octavio Getino had to work on this monumental film in an almost clandestine way, and smuggled the master negative out of the country one roll at a time so as to avoid the risk of it being destroyed by the repressive order. While a few copies were circulating underground in Argentina, the film became an international success, unprecedented for a Latin American film.

The dictatorial government of General Onganía, wanting, no doubt, to respond with all its might so that *La hora de los hornos* would not set a precedent, enacted law 18.019, which stated, in part, that "all films that compromise national security or that somehow affect the country's relations with friendly nations, or that damage the interests of the state's fundamental institutions" would be banned. In short, the law did not allow any criticism of the domestic or foreign policies of the dictatorship. But the law did not take progressive filmmakers working within the popular struggle by surprise. No law had given birth to the kind of cinema they made, and no law could put an end to it. Solanas and Getino adopted a clear position with regard to this law. In an article published in January 1969 in a publication of the *CGT* (*Confederación General de Trabajores*, the national trade union), they stated that "censorship, like any other form of repression, constitutes for the system implementing it a mechanism of self defence. It reveals, in one way or another, its weakness."

The main danger of the new law was not what it might actually prohibit but the effect it might have on less than totally committed directors. "The threat hovering over Argentine cinema," Solanas and Getino wrote, "is not so much this law but the lack of determination of some filmmakers, their self-censorship: the fears of those who, so as not to be left out of the mainstream, are already memorizing the law, adopting all their projects to its word — in short, devising new ways to avoid old traps."

"Doesn't this law in fact signal our movement's birth?" asked Solanas and Getino, prophetically, for from that time on the popular resistance intensified, harassing the dictatorship and forcing it into a corner. In the film industry, the censors showed their clumsy hand here and there, banning in 1970, for example, such films as Fellini's *Satyricon* and Pasolini's *Teorema*. The latter had already obtained authorization to be shown, albeit with cuts, but these proved insufficient. The day after the premiere, the police visited the theatres and seized all the prints, one by one. A special law was passed a few days later prohibiting the film's exhibition in Argentina. The Minister of the Interior, to justify the action, invoked "the national life-style," "moral principles," "the foundations of the family unit," etc. Later that same month, it was Fellini's turn, when his film was banned because of its "general theme."

In 1970 the filmmaker Daniel Mallo made *Ni vendecores ni vencidos?* (Neither Vanquished nor Victors?), a documentary full of archival footage from the period of Perón's first presidencies, from 1946 to 1955. The title of the film comes from a phrase uttered by General Lonardi immediately after the overthrow of Perón in 1955. Mallo worked for over two years researching and editing the film, but when it was finally ready to be shown, it was banned by virtue of law 226/71, which had declared a state of siege in Argentina. The film was shown, however, in Montevideo and Punta del Este in Uruguay, where many Argentines had a chance to see it. It received an award at the Bilbao Film Festival and was finally seen publicly in Argentina in late 1971.

That same year, Raymundo Gleyzer's film *México: la revolución congelada* (Mexico: The Frozen Revolution) was banned at the request of the Mexican Ambassador to Argentina. The film had been popular at the festivals of Cannes, Locarno and Manheim, but this was not taken into account.

Among the national films that could not be seen through the normal system, and were distributed through underground circuits, was the interesting documentary *Ya es tiempo de violencia* (Now's the Time for Violence). At about the same time, the Fourth International Festival of Documentary and Experimental Film took place in Argentina, sponsored by the Catholic University and co-sponsored by the OAS (Organization of American States) and UNESCO. Here too the censors were kept busy. Theoretically, their work should have been kept to a minimum, as most of the films were provided under the auspices of embassies. Those that came directly to the festival from abroad had to pass through the censor board. The censors prohibited the exhibition of two Chilean films (*Desnutrición infantil* — Infant Malnutrition, by Alvaro Ramírez and *Hermanida la victoria*, by Douglas Hübner) as well as the Argentine film *Muerte y pueblo* (Death and the People) by Nemesio Juarez.

Not only films of a political or socially critical nature were victimized by the censors in this period. In 1969, Héctor Olivera made *Los neuróticos* (The Neurotics), a satirical comedy that attempted to repeat the commercial success of an earlier film, *Psexoanalisis*. The censors cut a few scenes and made Olivera substitute *Los neuróticos* for the original title, *Los psexoanalizados*. Despite the cuts and modifications, the film was banned, but it was approved a year later after a change in personnel at the censor board. A similar case was that of *Ufa con el sexo* (Enough of Sex), made by Rodolfo Kuhn. If filmmakers believed they could avoid the censor by making apolitical films with great commercial appeal, they were mistaken. Kuhn's film was banned on the grounds that it breached the law that prohibited depictions "contrary to the national lifestyle or the cultural standards of the Argentine community."

There isn't an Argentine filmmaker who hasn't had to protect his or her films from the censor. A case worth mentioning is that of Gerardo Vallejo, a member of the *Cine Liberación* group. Vallejo studied at the Santa Fé film school under Birri, where he made the short film *Azucar* (Sugar). Later on he made *Las cosas ciertas* (Sure Things) and collaborated with Fernando Solanas and Octavio Getino on *La hora de los hornos*. Soon afterward he began his most ambitious personal project: *El camino hacia la muerte del Viejo Reales* (Old Man Reales' Road to Death), a study through one family of the lives of workers in the Tucumán region. Given the situation in Argentina in 1970, Vallejo opted to finish the film in Europe. On his return the film was, obviously, prohibited although it did circulate underground. Despite the fact that it had been awarded some prizes in Europe (or maybe because of this), he was persecuted by the authorities. "The film," recalls Vallejo, "was subversive in the eyes of the authorities, and as such had to be silenced, while it became a means of expression for the workers, who assumed it as their own."

The struggle that ensued on behalf of *El camino* was successful in obtaining authorization for the film to circulate freely. The working class of Tucumán mobilized around *FOTIA*, the sugar industry workers' association. At the end of a meeting attended by over a thousand workers, a demonstration was organized and they marched through the streets of Tucumán to the main government buildings, where the workers displayed placards that read, for example, "We demand to be recognized through the exhibition of this film." The media covered these events and finally, after two months of popular pressure, the film was passed. Later, with the return of Perón to power in 1973, Vallejo gained access to the files of the film institute, where he found a thick dossier on his film.

Before then, however, Vallejo would have to face the censor again, in 1972. At the time he was working on short documentaries for Tucumán regional television, for a series called *Testimonios tucumanos* (Testimonies from Tucumán). In November of that year, Perón returned to the country from his years of exile and Vallejo went to the airport to record his arrival. The program was cancelled by executives at the television station. A short time later though, *FOTIA* offered money to Vallejo to film *Testimonios de la reconstrucción* (Testimonies from the Reconstruction). For the first time a popular organization had financed the production of a film in Argentina.

Two Very Productive Years

Upon Perón's return to power in 1973, a period of democracy began that benefitted the film industry. The government allowed the uncut versions of such films as *La hora de los hornos, El camino* and *Operación masacre* (Operation Massacre, by Jorge Cedrón, 1972) to be screened in Argentina. The filmmakers grouped around *Cine Liberación*, who had issued a document called "Ways to Break the Dependency of the National Film Industry," were able to convert the its theories into a working program. In 1973, Octavio Getino was asked by the Minister of Education, Dr. Taiana, to head the film censor board. Getino replaced the omnipresent Ramiro de la Fuente, who had headed the organization for a decade under the repressive governments of Generals Organía, Levingston and Lanusse. Getino restructured the board and appointed representative figures from different sectors: psychologists and psychoanalysts such as Hernán Kesselman and Antonio Caparrós; sociologists such as Alcira Argumedo and Jorge Carpio; film critics such as Augustín Mahieu and Edmundo Eichelbaum; and filmmakers such as Rodolfo Kuhn and Humberto Ríos. He also invited representatives of the *CGT*, the national trade union, to sit on the board, a move that had no precedent in the history of Argentine film censorship.

Getino authorized the release of all the films that had previously been banned for political reasons, such as Costa Gavras' *State of Siege*, and others that had been banned for "moral" reasons, like Pasolini's *The Decameron* and Bertolucci's *Last Tango in Paris*. In the interview that follows, Getino explains in detail the characteristics of his tenure and the events he foresaw occuring had the democratic process continued.*

That process, though short-lived, permitted the production of films that had been impossible to make before Perón's return, and would again be impossible to make after 1975. Worth mentioning are *Quebracho* by Ricardo Wulicher, which depicts the British imperialism of the 1920s through a view of a resource extraction company, and *La Patagonia rebelde* (Rebellion in Patagonia) by Héctor Olivera. Other important films made during this period include *La Raulito* (Tomboy Paula) by Lautaro Murúa and *La tregua* (The Truce) by Sergio Renán, based on the novel by the Uruguyan writer Mario Benedetti.

At the same time, several radical film groups were active. The best known, apart from *Cine Liberación*, was *Cine Grupo de la Base* (The Grassroots Film Group), headed by Raymundo

---

* In that interview, which is not reproduced here, Getino explains how the censorship board worked under his direction. It classified films instead of banning them; sometimes these classifications were very pointed, as was the case with the Italian film the board labelled racist. The Argentine distributor appealed for a complete ban so it could get back the money paid for Argentine distribution rights; this was granted, the only time the board banned a film under Getino. The board also experimented with public classification sessions, fielding questions from the public after viewing a film and classifying it. [ed.]

Gleyzer, who had made several short films after studying with the Argentine ethnographic filmmaker Jorge Prelorán. He had also made a full length film in Mexico in 1971, *México: la revolución congelada*. In 1972 *Cine Grupo de la Base* produced *Los traidores* (The Traitors), a sharp criticism of corruption in the union bureaucracy.

In 1973-1974 there was talk in Argentina of a "New Argentine Cinema," and this was a valid expression. The conditions were present that allowed not only for the development of a more vigorous film industry, but for more personal experimentation as well. Even a wave of underground cinema appeared, represented by filmmakers such as Julio Ludueña, Edgardo Cozarinsky and Miguel Bejo. Ludueña made a feature called *Alianza para el progreso* (Alliance for Progress). Cozarinsky made ... (*Puntos suspendidos* — Dot Dot Dot) and Bejo made a disconcerting experimental film called *La familia unida esperando la llegada de Hallowyn* (The United Family Awaits the Arrival of Hallowe'en).

During that same period, Solanas and Getino completed an ambitious documentary they had begun in 1971, when they had filmed interviews with Perón in his exile in Madrid. Solanas and Getino accosted Perón with hundreds of questions on Peronism, Argentina and liberation movements in Latin America. They edited the results into two parts: the first, lasting 140 minutes, was called *Actualización política y doctrinaria para la toma del poder* (Political and Theoretical Renewal Towards the Taking of Power), and the second, three hours in length, was *La revolución justicialista* (The Justicialist Revolution). Both films were shown mainly to grassroots Peronist groups and remain documents of the political history of Argentina. After this, Getino began to work on a film for RAI (Radio-Televisione Italiana), *El familiar* (The Relative), based on a northern Tucumán legend. In 1972 Solanas began to film *Los hijos de Fierro* (The Children of Fierro), which he finished in exile in Europe in 1977 and which was not seen in Argentina until after the 1983 elections.

The Return to Darkness

The military coup of 1976 was preceded by a period of violence which underscored the changes underway in the country's power structure. Paramilitary organizations like the Triple A began to act with total impunity. In December 1974, several bombs exploded in the cinemas where Norman Jewison's *Jesus Christ Superstar* was showing. A few days before, the theatre that was showing the play of the same name had been attacked, and a devastating fire had followed. In July 1974, the film actor Julio Troxler, who had appeared in *La hora de los hornos, Operación masacre* and *Los hijos de Fierro*, was machine gunned by the Triple A. In September of that year this neo-fascist organization circulated a list of artists and intellectuals "sentenced to die."

The filmmakers who had been politically active during the democratic period were persecuted, jailed, and tortured, and many others left the country. The Triple A "invited" Fernando Solanas to seek refuge in Europe, Getino in Peru and later in Mexico, Gerardo Vallejo in Panama and later in Spain, Jorge Cedrón in France, etc. Less politically committed filmmakers, like Leopoldo Torre Nilsson, had censorship problems from then on. Torre Nilsson was in Spain in April 1976 when his new film *Piedra libre* (Home Free) was banned; he declared that he would not return to Argentina. In May Raymundo Gleyzer was kidnapped from his home by a paramilitary group. For months there was no news of his whereabouts until he was seen by chance in a torture cell near the Ezeiza airport, a captive of paramilitary groups that were a direct arm of the military government, in charge of the most foul and repulsive repression. Gleyzer was last seen in June 1976, in an appalling physical and mental state. Like other prisoners, he had been kept naked all the time, subjected to beatings and tortured with fire and electricity. The U.S. based Emergency Committee to Defend Latin American Filmmakers, formed by well-known representatives of the North American film industry, denounced this situation. Gleyzer's mother, Sara, desperately appealed to the government for permission to see her son. Filmmakers from all over the world appealed to the Argentine authorities, who probably threw the letters in the garbage. The greatest Italian filmmakers, Antonioni, Ferreri, Zavattini, Rosi, Rossellini, etc., sent a telegram to Alejandro Orfila (himself an Argentine), the Secretary General of the OAS, asking for his support, but almost every hope of seeing Gleyzer alive again has been lost.

A few days before Gleyzer's disappearance, the filmmaker Diego Bonacina was also kidnapped in Buenos Aires, this time by agents of the Federal Police. Bonacina had studied at the film school of Santa Fé and began working professionally in 1966 when he was in charge of photography on several short films. After 1967 he worked in Chile as a Director of Photography for Raúl Ruiz (*Tres tristes tigres* — Three Sad Tigers), Aldo Francia (*Valparaiso mi amor* — Valparaiso My Love) and other well-known Chilean filmmakers. He taught cinema in the film school of the University of Chile (Valparaiso) and made several short films for Chile Films. During the 1973 coup in Chile, Bonacina was detained in the National Stadium and was deported to Argentina. After his kidnapping in Buenos Aires he was detained without charges and later released.

A worse fate has befallen some well-known writers and screenwriters. One is Haroldo Conti, author of *En vida* (Alive) and *Mascaró*, and winner of the 1975 *Casa de las Américas* prize. He wrote the novel *Operación masacre*, the basis of Jorge Cedrón's film. In a UNESCO meeting in February 1977, more than one hundred filmmakers and critics signed a petition on behalf of the imprisoned filmmakers in Argentina and Chile. Among the signatories were Alain Robbe-Grillet, Dusan Makavejev, Peter Foldes, Sarah Maldoror, Guy Hennebelle, Marcel Martin and Noël Burch.

The situation of the "disappeared" in Argentina has worsened and it is not limited to filmmakers and intellectuals. According to Amnesty International, more than thirty thousand people have disappeared since 1976. The U.S. magazine *Time* reported in September 1979 that the Argentine authorities were stealing files on the disappeared from the offices of the League for Human Rights.

All this repression has destroyed the film industry. Argentina has not won any prizes in film festivals and produces hardly any interesting films. Filmmakers even suspect that Argentine labs are under the control of the Junta, to monitor their work.

Argentine filmmakers have not been able to work underground either, although some good films have been produced under very difficult conditions. These films are usually finished outside the country. Some examples are *Bandido como Jesús* (A Bandit Like Jesus), featuring interviews with several progressive priests; *Las vacas sagradas* (The Sacred Cows); *Las tres A son las tres armas* (The Triple A are the Three Armed Forces), produced by *Cine Grupo de la Base* and based on the text of an open letter from the writer Rodolfo Walsh to the military Junta before his disappearance. One of the most important films made during this period, which will not be shown in Argentina, is *Resistir* (To Resist). A documentary produced in 1978 by "Julian Calinki" (an alias of Jorge Cedrón), it is a rigorous analysis of the Peronist movement. The body of the film is a long interview with the leader of the *Monteneros**, Mario Firmenich. The quality of the documentary footage, the vitality of the editing, and the sharpness of the critical analysis makes this film one of the most penetrating documentaries produced in Argentina.

The writer Julio Cortázar saw the film in Paris and wrote: "Among the films that attempt to trace the historical and social evolution of Argentina in the last decade, *Resistir* seems to me a complete success. This type of film sometimes runs the risk of being schematic or stereotyped or purely and simply demagogic. In the case of *Resistir*, the objectivity displayed is especially startling because it is mainly a long interview with Firmenich, leader of the *Monteneros*. Instead of excesses and vehemences, Firmenich displays all through his discussion a remarkable rigour. He examines the sad process of the progressive decay of Argentine political and social life, and makes an effort to situate each period in its true context. As a *Montenero* he does not hesitate to criticize the corruption of those Peronists in power after the old leader's return, and attacks the betrayal of the masses by the Peronist Right, who had promised to represent and defend them. *Resistir* is a document of genuine clarity

* The *Monteneros* were a group of radical Peronists, mostly young university students and activists, who took up armed struggle against the military dictatorship in the years preceding Perón's return in 1973. Afterward, they were the victims of repression carried out by the Peronist right wing, particularly after Perón's death in 1974. [ed.]

on the repression and on the true origin of this violence, which the Junta blames on 'professional subversives.' "

Translated by Al Cedrez and Beatriz Munárriz

Octavio Getino (photograph by Alfonso Gumucio Dagron)

Some Notes on the Concept of a "Third Cinema"
Octavio Getino

Octavio Getino, born in Spain but a resident of Argentina from the early 1950s until his exile in 1976, was a co-founder of the radical Argentine film collective Cine Liberación, *which had a great influence on the development of the "New Latin American Cinema" and on radical filmmaking around the world.*

In this article, excerpted from his book Notas sobre cine argentino y latinoamericano *(1984), Getino reflects on the evolution of the group in the context of the changes in Argentine social and political life since 1966. In that year, he and Fernando Solanas began filming* La hora de los hornos *(The Hour of the Furnaces), and widespread resistance against military rule broke out. The violent swings in Argentine political life during the decade following the start of work on* La hora de los hornos — *from military dictatorship to populist democracy and back to military rule again — are reflected in the theories and practices of* Cine Liberación. *Getino himself went from being an underground filmmaker to the head of the film classification board under Perón, and was exiled from Argentina after the military coup of 1976.*

With the return of Perón in 1973, the group renounced their "guerrilla cinema" tactics and began to produce features for commercial release. This, Getino argues here, was consistent with the group's goal of establishing a vital and autonomous national film industry, and was the logical outcome of the dovetailing of the group's radical populism with the freedom brought by Perón's return to power.

Like the previous article by Alfonso Gumucio Dagron, Some Notes on the Concept of a "Third Cinema" *was written at the height of the Argentine military dictatorship (during Getino's exile in Peru in the late 1970s), and thus his comments do not reflect the changes in Argentina since the elections of 1983.*

1. Antecedents

The first reference to the concept of a "Third Cinema" appeared in the Cuban film journal *Cine Cubano* in March 1969, in a report of an interview with members of the Argentine *Cine Liberación* group. At that time, the group maintained that "there is a growing need for a 'third cinema', one that would not fall into the trap of trying to engage in a dialogue with those who have no interest in doing so. It would be a cinema of aggression, a cinema that would put an end to the irrationality that has come before it, an *agit* cinema. This does not mean that filmmakers should take on exclusively political or revolutionary themes, but that their films would thoroughly explore all aspects of life in Latin America today. This cinema, revolutionary in both its formulation and its consciousness, would invent a new cinematographic language, in order to create a new consciousness and a new social reality."*

A few months later, in October 1969, the article "Toward a Third Cinema: Notes and Experiences Regarding the Development of a Liberation Cinema in the Third World" appeared in the journal *Tricontinental*, published in Paris. With these notes, the group hazarded a few theoretical definitions of a Third Cinema's objectives and methodology. Certain ambiguities were left in this formulation of the theory, however, so these were clarified during the *Encuentro de Cineastas Latino-americanos* (Latin American Filmmakers' Conference) held in Viña del Mar, Chile, with the publication of the article "Militant Cinema: An Internal Category of Third Cinema". These publications had a significant effect on young filmmakers, not only in Latin America and the Third World, but also in the highly developed countries, such as the United States, Canada, France, and Italy,

---

* *Cine Liberación* identified three major currents in world cinema: the first was the classical cinema of Hollywood and the major European film industries; the second, a personal *auteur* cinema that grew up in opposition to this cinema but was itself marked by various political contradictions and artistic and productive compromises; and the "Third Cinema" which, because of its collective production, parallel distribution (which emphasized audience discussion) and direct confrontation of political events, would overcome the limitations of an *auteur* cinema. [ed.]

and they were reprinted in books and specialized journals. From that time on, *Cine Liberación*, as a group, did not return to these themes. Its principal members — Fernando Solanas, Gerardo Vallejo, and the author of these notes — did, however, continue to discuss them in articles, interviews and debates published in specialized journals around the world.

It is essential that I note these antecedents in order to analyse — in a provisory and strictly personal manner — the value these theories on the Third Cinema, elaborated 10 years ago, may have today.

The National Context as Generator of Theory and Practice

The attempt to create a Third Cinema in Argentina was bound up in our own particular historical and political circumstances, marked during the last years of the 1960's by the increase in the levels of organization and mobilization of popular resistance movements. An increasing cohesion between the middle and working classes also developed during this period of military rule, culminating in 1973 with the resounding electoral victory of the *Frente Justicialista de Liberación*, led by the Peronist movement and supported by every progressive sector in the country.

The practical work of *Cine Liberación* was thus conditioned by the simultaneous growth of national resistance movements and the effort to democratize the country. This situation defined the orientation and theories of the group. The language of the films produced by the members of the group was similarly informed by the political reality of Argentina as well. In opposition to the prevailing notion of an *auteur* cinema, we developed this notion of a Third Cinema, an *agit* cinema, a cinema made collectively. We didn't fully realize at the time the extent to which the Argentine reality of the late 1960's defined the content and form of our work and its parallel theoretical elaboration. In turn, our work was destined to contribute to the development and liberation of the country, as well as to certain debates in the history of film. This is not to deny whatever universal value certain aspects of the theory may have had; it is worth emphasizing, however, that the value of theories such as these is always dependent on the terrain in which the praxis is carried out. Any attempt to consider an ideological product universal would be erroneous without consideration of the national context at its root.

Practice as the Generator of Theory

In order to understand fully the sense of the Third Cinema program, we must note that its theoretical component arose after, and not before, the practical work of making films, that is to say, after the production and distribution of *La hora de los hornos* (The Hour of the Furnaces), directed by Solanas, which was begun in 1966 and finished in 1968.

Both Solanas and myself, while making this film, amassed a considerable amount of theoretical material. It was for our own use, as reflections on our ongoing practical work. It was this material that we drew upon when we developed the theories that were published between 1969 and 71.

It is difficult to imagine the subsequent international exposure of these theories had the film not existed. It was only through the existence of the film that we were able to refute the opposition of critics to our theories.

With this film, we demonstrated for the first time that it was possible to produce and distribute a film within a non-liberated country with the specific aim of contributing to the political process of liberation. To do this, we had to develop a different way of using film than that which had existed until that time. It thus remains difficult even today to separate the concept of Third Cinema from the film *La hora de los hornos*, which demonstrates the interdependence of theory and practice. It is this practice which should constitute the principal theme of analysis today as it stimulated, even determined, the kinds of theories we put forward 10 years ago.

The Social Context as Mediator

The production and distribution of *La hora de los hornos* was possible, as I have already noted, because of the strong offensive of a popular resistance movement against a military power in full retreat. This opposition movement, basically led by the Peronist party, had a strong national tradition and organizational structure, through the trade unions and on the local community level. This facilitated the distribution of alternative films via decentralized parallel circuits, which would have been impossible to maintain under different political circumstances. Even then, the continuation of this practice required a theoretical base capable of guiding its development.

Another factor that should be noted in this discussion of the theories surrounding the Third Cinema movement is the social origin of the filmmakers in the *Cine Liberación* group. By the mid-1960's, as the economic development policies of the military rulers proved disastrous, the increasingly impoverished middle class began to seek a way out of the impasse in any manner available to them. During this same period, the well-organized working class successfully frustrated repeated attempts to fundamentally subvert certain democratic institutions in the Argentine political process. It was also a time when events abroad, particularly the Cuban Revolution, were having an effect in Argentina. This revolution was being idealized, even by the middle class, into a universal model for political organization in Latin America.

Naturally, the working class, hardened by decades of struggle in which it was the principal — and often solitary — protagonist, experienced this period differently than the middle class. Historically, the working class exercised a hegemony on the process of national liberation. The middle class could only hope to join this revolutionary process, from which it had previously kept its distance at every critical historical juncture.

La hora de los hornos, and the other films made by *Cine Liberación*, must be analysed in this context, that of middle class intellectuals caught up in insurrectionary mobilizations, influenced by the cultural-political traditions of the working class movement, but still embodying contradictions inherited from the neo-colonization of Argentina.

For my part, I believe that we too were not free of this dynamic. *Cine Liberación* was, before anything else, our fusion as intellectuals with the working class's reality. This determined the tentative and inconclusive nature of our proposals. "Until now", we emphasized in "Toward a Third Cinema", "we have put forward practical proposals but only loose ideas — just a sketch of the hypotheses that were born of our first film,

La hora de los hornos. We thus don't pretend to present them as a sole or exclusive model, but only as ideas which may be useful in the debate over the use of film in non-liberated countries".

2. The Theory and Practice of Third Cinema in Argentina

We can identify three principal stages in the work of the *Cine Liberación* group:
   i)   that of the group's formation and initial activities, as part of the resistance against the Argentine military governments of Onganía, Levingston, and Lanusse;
   ii)   that of its open collaboration with the democratic and populist government that ruled in 1973 and 74, until the death of the President of the country, Juan Domingo Perón;
   iii) that of its withdrawal to a new form of resistance, which is the current stage, the stage of exile.

The First Stage, 1966-1970/71

The first stage of the group's activities is delineated, approximately, by the years 1966 and 1970/71. This was the period during which the work with the greatest international impact was produced. I refer here primarily to the film *La hora de los hornos*, directed by Solanas, on which I collaborated as co-author: this film established the base from which the group would work, both within Argentina and abroad. When the film was finished, we began the other, no less important task of setting up parallel distribution circuits for the film to circulate through trade unions and community and Peronist Youth organizations.

During this period young filmmakers began to organize, together with Peronist activists and other progressive groups, giving rise to testimonial films and documentaries about what was happening in Argentina at that time. The *CGT* (*Confederación General de Trabajadores* — The National Trade Union), for example, put out the newsreel *Cineinformes de la CGT de los argentinos* at this time.

As work progressed on the practical levels of production and distribution, the group published its three major theoretical pieces: *La cultura nacional, el cine, y La hora de los hornos* (National Culture, Cinema, and The Hour of the Furnaces, Fernando Solanas and Octavio Getino, *Cine Cubano* no. 56/57, Havana, March 1969); *Hacia un tercer cine* (Toward a Third Cinema, Solanas and Getino, *Tricontinental* no. 13, OSPAAAL, Paris, October 1969); and *Cine militante: una categoría interna del tercer cine* (Militant Cinema: An Internal Category of Third Cinema, Solanas and Getino, mimeograph, Viña del Mar, 1971). The group also published material in the periodicals *Notas de Cine Liberación* and *Sobres de cultura y liberación* (On Culture and Liberation), the latter published by a united front of visual artists, students, and political activists with similar objectives to our own. We also made films throughout this period, of course, which were always excluded from conventional distribution circuits. It was only through the popular organizations that we were able to distribute them.

The Second Stage, 1971-1974

This stage, which saw our work having fewer international repercussions, led instead to our films really taking root in national life. We ran the risk of having our films censored and began to make films intended for commercial release through normal distribution channels. The first film to do this was Gerardo Vallejo's *El camino hacia la muerte del Viejo Reales* (Old Man Reales' Road to Death, 1970). I made *El familiar* (The Relative, 1973) and Solanas made *Los hijos de Fierro* (The Children of Fierro, 1977, begun in 1972). Similar films, made outside our group but from the same "liberation cinema" perspective, should be noted as well, especially *Operación masacre* (Operation Massacre, 1972), by Jorge Cedrón.

Numerous short films were made in each of the regional centres of the country. In Tucumán, for example, Vallejo made *Testimonios tucumanos* (Testimonies from Tucumán) and later *Testimonios de la reconstrucción* (Testimonies from the Reconstruction) which were screened on the regional TV network operated by the university of that province.

This new approach required us to formulate new ideas in our written material as well. The magazine *Cine y Liberación* appeared in 1972 and reflected the popular resistance that was by then poised to take power. It was also during this period that we made two important documentaries in Madrid with Perón for the Peronist movement, *Actualización política y doctrinaria para la toma del poder* (Political and Theoretical Renewal Towards the Taking of Power) and *La revolución justicialista* (The Justicialist Revolution). In order to distribute these films, we used — and expanded — the parallel circuits we had developed for *La hora de los hornos*. The demand for these two films, particularly the latter, in fact surpassed the demand for this earlier film, and we made more than fifty 16mm copies of *La revolución justicialista*.

This double-edged production strategy, with some films aimed at commercial audiences and others made for the parallel circuits, was accompanied by the organization of filmmakers, and not only of activists but of others who were part of the mainstream industry but who were being politicized by the events of the period. At this time, our group was composed of filmmakers, critics, actors, independent producers, short filmmakers, technicians and film workers, who were united by the one cohesive factor of the pressing need to develop a project of national liberation, both for the country and for its cinema. With the liberation of the country in 1973, we were able to take part in the formulation of new policies in the film industry. It was in this period that I was asked to head *El Ente de Califacación*, the censor board, a task I shared with all those concerned with the real development of our film industry.*

The group's work in this period did not go long undenounced,

---

* During his one year term as head of Argentina's film censor board, Getino turned the organization upside-down with his populist Peronist policies. Also discussed in Alfonso Gumucio Dagron's article on film censorship elsewhere in this volume, these included: approving all domestic and foreign films which had previously been banned for political or moral reasons; substituting classification for censorship, a process that included identifying and labelling films that were racist, etc.; and changing the composition of the board from one dominated by religious and moral extremists to one with representatives of the film industry, the country's trade unions, the social science professions, and the general public (to the point of experimenting with public classification sessions). [ed.]

by the extreme Left before anyone else, who accused us of being "opportunists" and "bureaucrats." Afterwards, the extreme Right joined in, but with different, and undoubtedly more forceful arguments. As far as the Left is concerned, there were some extreme tendencies at work in the country at this time, which had little popular support. Their leaders confused tactics with strategy and the means with the end. Their film activity they called "guerrilla cinema," which appropriated our theories of several years earlier and adopted them as a dogmatic Bible. They saw in our work a supposed retreat into pro-Government propaganda, not distinguishing between support for the Armed Forces and support for a government elected by 70% of the people. This ultra-left offensive, launched in order to create obstacles to the democratic process, attempted to initiate a "popular revolutionary war," which actually led to miniscule ghettoized groups as alienated from the national will as the paramilitary groups of the far Right.

The Third Stage, 1974 —

From 1974 on, after the death of Perón, the political project that the majority of the people had set in motion a year earlier began to falter. The imperialist offensive, visible in the events around us in Uruguay, Bolivia, and Chile,* coincided with this weakening, which unfolded rapidly. It became clear that the force and cohesion of the popular movements in these countries — and in Argentina — were not as strong as we had imagined. In addition, the international solidarity promised us by those who make revolutionary chatter a way of life failed to material-ize, coming only after the military coup of 1976.†

We are now living in a time when the repression is so severe that we can't make films in Argentina either above ground or underground. To speak of a "guerrilla cinema," for example, would be absurd. To attempt to make that kind of cinema in

---

* There were military coups in Bolivia in 1971 and in Chile and Uruguay in 1973 (the latter country's first coup ever). [ed.]

† A reference to the fact that after the military coup of 1976 in Argen-tina and throughout the murderous regime of General Videla, the USSR strengthened its trade and diplomatic relations with the country. [ed.]

Argentina today would undermine the position of the popular classes rather than strengthen it. *Cine Liberación* thus abandoned the use of "guerrilla" tactics, which to our mind had value during the popular offensive but ceased to do so after 1973. It was precisely during this latter period that "militant cinema", at least that form of it practiced by us, in fact deepened its militancy by involving itself in the everyday political tasks of the masses, renouncing all forms of "vanguardism" that were outside the newly created democratic process.

As we had established during the earlier stage of our work, we prefer to err with the people rather than to take the "correct line" without them. It was not a coincidence, then, that just as we launched *La hora de los hornos*, the orthodox Marxist Left, in Paris and Buenos Aires, now joined the Right and attacked our position. We were "populist" and "fascist" to the former, yet "subversive" and "communist" to the latter. Both groups used essentially the same intimidation tactics and differed only in their choice of adjectives to describe us.

The change in our practical course during this period modified our theoretical positions, although these were not set out in written form as they were during the earlier stage. Instead, we strove to realize some of the ideas we had formulated earlier, particularly our search for new film languages capable of expressing with more rigour and insight our social reality. This involved opening up to new genres and styles which could not be classified as documentary films. We wanted to contribute to the de-colonization of our country's movie screens and thus put an end to the cultural and economic dependency of our film industry.

We thus entered into a period of critical revision and autocritique. To do so in the realm of practice seems to me the best method, in that the autocritique is constantly being verified by the actualization of ideas, ideas that are always tied to the necessities of the national reality and to the question of political strategy.

Translated by Tim Barnard and Alfredo Marchevsky

Lucas, His Friends
Julio Cortázar

Julio Cortázar was perhaps Argentina's greatest novelist until his death in Paris in 1984. Despite his not having lived in Argentina for thirty years, he retained his interest in Argentine themes and characters. His short story Blow-Up *was the inspiration for the Michaelangelo Antonioni film of the same title, and his work has been frequently put on the screen by Argentine filmmakers.*

"Lucas, His Friends" is excerpted from Un tal Lucas *(A Certain Lucas), a book of short anecdotes (Lucas, His Disconcertedness; Lucas, His Modesty; Lucas, His Spanish Classes; etc.) about the life of a certain Lucas, Cortázar's alter ego.*

Jorge Cedrón, one of the friends described here, was an Argentine filmmaker and part of the Argentine exile community in Paris in the late 1970s (which, along with Cortázar, included the filmmakers Fernando Solanas and Edgardo Cozarinsky). Cedrón's most successful and controversial film, Operación masacre *(Operation Massacre, 1972) recounted the slaughter of Peronist activists at the hands of the military, shortly after the coup that overthrew Perón in 1955.*

The list of cronies is large and varied, but who can say why it occurs to him now to think especially about the Cedróns, and thinking about the Cedróns means so many things that he doesn't know where to begin. The only thing in Lucas's favor is that he doesn't know all of the Cedróns, only three of them, but who can say whether or not that's in his favor in the end. He's been given to understand that the brothers add up to a sum of six or nine, in any case, he knows three, so hang on, we're off and running.

These three Cedróns consist of the musician Tata, Jorge the filmmaker, and Alberto the painter. Trying to separate them is something else again, but when they decide to get together and they invite you for some meat tarts, then they really are death in three volumes.

What I can tell you about getting there, from the street you can hear a kind of uproar on one of the upper floors, and if you pass one of their Parisian neighbours you can see on their faces that corpselike paleness of people who have witnessed a phenomenon that goes beyond the parameters of that strait-laced and muffed race. No need to ask what floor the Cedróns are on because the noise guides you up the stairs to one of the doors that looks less like a door than the others and also gives the impression of being red-hot because of what's going on inside, to the point that you'd better not knock too long because you'll scorch your knuckles. Of course, the door is most likely wide open, since the Cedróns are also going in and out and, besides, why close a door that gives such good ventilation from the stairway.

What happens as you enter renders coherent description impossible, because as soon as you cross the threshold there's a little girl who grabs you by the knees and covers your topcoat with spittle, and at the same time a little boy who has climbed up onto the bookcase in the foyer dives at your neck like a kamikaze, so that if you had the vague idea of coming with a bottle of cheap red, the instantaneous result is a gaudy puddle on the carpet. This doesn't bother anyone, of course, because at that same moment the wives of the Cedróns appear from different rooms, and while one of them untangles you from the kids on top of you, the others sop up the unfortunate burgundy with some rags that probably go back to the times of the Crusades. With all this, Jorge has told you in detail the plots of two or three novels that he intends to film, Alberto holds back two other children armed with bows and arrows and, what is worse, endowed with singular marksmanship, and Tata comes out of the kitchen wearing an apron that once knew the color white in its earliest days and which envelops him majestically from the armpits down, giving him a surprising resemblance to Mark Antony or any of the types who vegetate in the Louvre or work at being statues in parks. The great news proclaimed simultaneously by ten or twelve voices is that there are meat tarts, into the making of which went the participation of Tata's wife and Tata himself, but whose recipe has been considerably improved by Alberto, who is of the opinion that leaving Tata and his wife alone in the kitchen can only lead to the worst of catastrophes. As for Jorge, who for no reason will refuse to stay out of what is coming, he has already brought forth generous quantities of wine and everybody, once these tumultuous preliminaries have been resolved, settles onto the bed, onto the floor, or where there isn't a kid crying or peeing, which ends up as the same thing but at different levels.

A night with the Cedróns and their unselfish ladies (I say unselfish because if I were a woman and also the woman of one of the Cedróns, it would have been a long time back that the bread knife would have put a voluntary end to my suffering, but they not only don't suffer but are even worse than the Cedróns, something that delights me because it's good for someone to get the best of them from time to time, and I think the women get the best of them all the time), a night with the Cedróns is a kind of South American summary that explains and justifies the stupefied wonder with which Europeans attend to their music, their literature, their painting, and their movies or theatre. Now that I think of it, I remember something told me by the Quilapayúns, who are cronopios just as mad as the Cedróns, but musicians all, the question being whether for better or for worse. During a trip through Germany (the eastern one but I think the effects of the case would have been the same no matter which) the Quilapayúns decided to have an outdoor barbecue Chilean style, but to their general surprise they discovered that in that country you can't have a picnic in the woods without permission from the authorities. Permission isn't hard to get, one has to admit, and the police took it so seriously that at the time for lighting the fires and placing the creatures on their respective spits, a fire truck appeared, whose passengers spread out through the nearby woods and spent five hours making sure that the fire wouldn't spread through the Wagnerian firs and other plants that abound in Teutonic forests. If memory serves, several of those firemen ended up stuffing their guts, as befits the prestige of their calling, and that day there was a fraternizing that is unusual between those in uniform and civilians. It's true that the fireman's uniform is the least whorish of all uniforms, and on the day when with the help of millions of Quilapayúns and Cedróns we consign all South American uniforms to the trash can, the only ones saved will be firemen's and we'll even invent more handsome models for them so the lads will be happy while they put out fires or save poor ravished girls who have decided to jump in the river for want of something better.

With all this the meat tarts disappear with a speed worthy of people who look at each other with a fierce hatred because this fellow had seven and the other only five and at one of these points the coming and going of platters ceases and some poor fool suggests coffee, as if that were food. The ones who always seem the least interested are the kids, whose number will still be an enigma for Lucas, for as soon as one disappears behind a bed or into the hallway, two others burst out of a closet or slide down the trunk of a rubber plant until they sit smack in a platter full of meat tarts. These tots feign a certain disdain for such a noble Argentine product, under the pretext that their respective mothers have already nourished them as a precaution a half hour before, but judging from the way in which the meat tarts disappear, one can only be convinced that they're an important element in infantile metabolism, and that if Herod were there that night another cock would have crowed for us and Lucas, instead of twelve meat tarts, would have been able to eat seventeen, all, of course, with the necessary breaks for trips to the wine cellar for a couple of quarts, which, as is well known, settle protein.

Above, below, and in the midst of the meat tarts there reigns a clamor of declarations, questions, protests, laughs, and general displays of joy and love that creates an atmosphere alongside which a war council to Tehuelche or Mapuche Indians would resemble the wake for a law professor. From time to time raps can be heard on the ceiling, on the floor, and on the two adjoining walls, and almost always it is Tata (tenant of the apartment) who announces that it's only the neighbors, which doesn't make for the least cause for worry. The fact that it's one in the morning is no reason for aggrievement or anything else, because at two-thirty we go downstairs four steps at a time singing the tango lines *que te abrás en las paradas / con cafishos milon-*

gueros at the top of our lungs. There has already been sufficient time to solve most of the problems of the planet, we've agreed to screw more than four people who deserve it and how, date books have been filled with telephone numbers and addresses and get-togethers in cafés and other apartments, and tomorrow the Cedróns are going to split up because Alberto is going back to Rome, Tata is leaving with his quartet to sing in Poitiers, and Jorge is splitting for God knows where but always with his light meter in his hand and no holding him. It isn't of no use to add that Lucas goes home with the feeling that on his shoulders he has a sort of pumpkin filled with horseflies, Boeing 707s, and several superimposed solos by Max Roach. But what does he care about a hangover if down below there's some little hot thing that must be the meat tarts, and between down and up there's something even warmer still, a heart that repeats what fuckups, what fuckups, what glorious fuckups, what irreplaceable fuckups, crazy motherfuckers.

Translated by Gregory Rabassa

Jorge Cedrón died in Paris of a gunshot wound in 1980. The police concluded that it was self-inflicted; Cedrón's friends and associates insist he was assassinated by agents of the military Junta in Argentina.

Statement on Jorge Cedrón

Jorge Cedrón has died. A curtain of silence has fallen over his death. Just as Cedrón's films were dedicated to recounting a silenced history, we want to testify to our solidarity with his life and his death.

He made two short films: *La vereda de enfrente* and *El otro oficio*; and four features: *El habilitado, Por los senderos de la libertador, Operación masacre*, and *Tango*. He was forced to leave Argentina at the beginning of 1977, leaving behind a film, unfinished and probably destroyed. At the time of his death, he was preparing to film *Asilo*, a feature on exile.

With *El habilitado*, besides receiving invitations to European festivals, Cedrón won the Argentine film critic's prize. But the film was neglected by the Argentine film distribution monopolies. Without official help, Cedrón then set up alternative production and distribution methods.

And he filmed *Operación masacre*: a faithful reconstruction and analysis of the shooting of militant Peronists in 1956, by order of General Aramburu.

Because of its virtually clandestine production, its complexity, and its cost, it represented a real feat.

The significance of the film's political, human and popular resistance went beyond the incidents depicted and defied the very notion of military rule.

For Rodolfo Walsh, author of the book and screenplay, writer and journalist, today 'disappeared'; for Julio Troxler, a survivor of the massacre who played himself in the film, assassinated in 1974 by the Triple A*; for Armando Imaz, directorial assistant, murdered in 1977 by the Military Junta; for Jorge Cedrón, nicknamed the Tiger, who died in Paris because the bars of his own prison in exile became confused with those of the prisons where thousands of his Argentine brothers and sisters have died. *Operación masacre* was more than just a film. With their lives they have filled it with blood and truth.

Julio Cortázar
Jean-Paul Carrière
Anatole Dauman
Paco Ibañez
Jacqueline Lenoir
Antonio Segui

Translated by Tim Barnard

* The Triple A was the paramilitary "anti-communist" group formed by reactionary factions within the Peronist government after the death of Perón in 1974. It was the Triple A, in fact, that began the "dirty war" against dissidents that was intensified under the Junta that took power in 1976, and which was responsible for the deaths of several thousand of Argentina's 30,000 "missing". [ed.]

Partial Enchantments of Narrative:
Borges in/and/on Film
Edgardo Cozarinsky

In this article, expatriate Argentine filmmaker and critic Edgardo Cozarinsky discusses — in an appropriately Borgesian manner — the relationship between the work of renowned man of letters Jorge Luis Borges and the cinema. Before falling victim to an early blindness in the 1950s, Borges — a poet, literary critic, essayist and short story writer — was a big fan of the cinema.

This article is excerpted from the forthcoming English translation of Cozarinsky's book Borges en/y/sobre cine *(Borges in/and/on Film, Lumen, N.Y.). In the foreword to that book, Cozarinsky writes: "Borges' relationship with film has been as labyrinthine and surprising as his characters' relation to time, and this book attempts to inventory, on a necessarily provisional basis, the numerous, even contradictory aspects of this relationship.... While the 1981 Spanish edition was the first to respect the title I had originally chosen for the book, this present edition not only 'corrects, augments and updates' my book entitled* Borges y el cine, *which appeared in Argentina in 1974, it also includes material that had only appeared in the Italian edition (Il Formichiere, 1978) and other material added to the French edition (Albatros, 1979) and to various editions since. I think Borges would be pleased by the idea of a book whose different editions did not coincide, either in title or content."*

> *Writers have always wanted to create cinema*
> *on the blank page: to arrange all the*
> *elements and let thought roam among them.*
> Jean-Luc Godard, interviewed
> in *Cahiers du Cinema* 171,
> October 1965

Film — an *idea* of film, really — recurs in Borges's writing linked to the practice of narration, even to the possibility of attempting narration. Films also appear as reading matter, one among the countless motives for reflection lavished on us by the universe. The examples offered to Borges by films illustrate widely disparate themes: the hilarious response of a Buenos Aires audience to some scenes from *Hallelujah* and *Underworld* provokes his bitter commentary on "Our Impossibilities" (an article dating from 1931 and included in *Discusión* (Discussion) the following year but eliminated from the 1957 edition); von Sternberg gives him the chance to confirm a hypothesis about the workings of all story telling ("The Postulation of Reality" and "Narrative Art and Magic," both included in *Discusión*); Joan Crawford makes an appearance in the second of these essays and Miriam Hopkins in "History of Eternity" from the volume of the same title; "the impetuous film *Hallelujah*" provides one of the many results of bringing blacks to America that Borges enumerates in *Historia universal de la infamia* (Universal History of Infamy); the modest translator Edward William Lane yields a basis for Borges' comparison with Hollywood's then-rigid censorship code — "The Translators of the 1001 Nights," *Historia de la eternidad* (History of Eternity).

During the 1920s and 30s, Borges saw the mere distribution of images by means of film as an incalculable enrichment of life, perhaps because he knew how to recognize those images, even though they were fictitious — or above all, *because* they were fictitious? — signs of a broader context. In a digression, subsequently deleted when he revised *Discusión*, Borges refers in his 1929 essay "The Other Whitman" to the lack of communication between inhabitants of "the diverse Americas," and he proceeds to venture an opinion: it is "a lack of communication that films, with their direct presentation of destinies and their no less direct presentation of wills, tend to overcome." This catalogue of references could be extended effortlessly, but its sole importance is to establish the degree to which films were a habit for the young Borges, an accessible repertoire of allusions, which he consulted as frequently as the *Encyclopedia Britannica* or unpublished reality.

At that time, film represented to Borges the image of literature (or history or philosophy) as a single text fragmented into countless, even contradictory passages, which neither individually represented that text nor in combination exhausted it. With even greater ease than in those prestigious disciplines, this notion could come to life in the films Borges frequented and quoted from, with diminishing regularity after 1940: a cinema that in spite of Eisenstein and Welles could still seem an art unfettered by too many big names, a cinema that was, above all else, free of bibliographies and academies. Allardyce Nicoll, whose *Film and Theatre* (1936) Borges dismissed as an exercise in pedantry, presented himself as "well versed in libraries, erudite in card catalogues, sovereign in files," but "nearly illiterate in box-offices..."

In this cinematic realm, many obscure narrators practiced the "differing intonation of a few metaphors" ("The Sphere of Pascal," *Otras inquisiciones* — Other Inquisitions) whose history may be the history of the universe. "I think nowadays, while literary men seem to have neglected their epic duties, the epic has been saved for us, strangely enough, by the Westerns," Borges told Ronald Christ in an interview published in *The Paris Review* 40 (Winter/Spring 1967). "During this century," he said, the epic tradition has been saved for the world by, of all places, Hollywood." If Hollywood really was able to compile a film-text, both craftsmanlike and collective, as well as bearing comparison to the ancient sagas, then Borges' predilection for that text is, *horrible dictu*, sophisticated. In order to belittle the films that von Sternberg composed around Marlene Dietrich, Borges repeatedly defends von Sternberg's earlier action films; and, in the interview with Christ, he recalls that "when I saw the first gangster films of von Sternberg I remember that when there was anything epic about them — I mean Chicago gangsters dying bravely — well, I felt that my eyes were full of tears." But von Sternberg was neither Wellman nor Hawks nor Walsh — figures who, with greater credibility, might embody a cinematic scald. Obviously, Borges felt attracted by the stylization that von Sternberg imposed on his gangland characters, settings, and conventions, whose usual violence is less elliptical, less ironic than in films like *Underworld* or *The Docks of New York*.

It is no accident that von Sternberg is the only film director whom Borges assiduously refers to or that those references appear in his early studies of narrative technique included in *Discusión* as well as in the 1935 prologue to the *Historia universal de la infamia* where the epic invocation turns into an exercise of verbal legerdemain. In the 1954 prologue to that book, Borges writes: "Scaffolds and pirates populate it, and the word *infamy* blares in the title; but, behind all the tumult, there is nothing. The book is nothing more than appearance, nothing more than a surface of images, and for that very reason it may prove pleasurable." Films, of course, *are* that surface of images, and nothing can be found behind the words of any literary work; but to admit and flaunt one's working against the referential function of language is as skeptical and cultivated an attitude as nostalgia for epic or disdain for romantic individualism.

Less ascetic than Valéry, Borges put his distrust of the novel into practice. His impatience with mere length is well known: "It is an impoverishing and laborious extravagance to create long books, to extend into 500 pages an idea whose perfect oral expression takes a few minutes. A better procedure is to pretend that these books already exist and to offer a summary, a commentary" (Prologue to *El jardín de senderos que se bifurcan* — The Garden of Forking Paths). Such boldness destroys the very possibility of even approaching a genre that, in order to develop a character and to proportion its episodes, requires a necessarily unhurried orchestration of specific circumstances and trivial information. Borges has also explained that Hawthorne's talent lent itself more to the short story than to the novel because he preferred to start from situations rather than characters: "Hawthorne first imagined a situation, perhaps involuntarily, and afterward looked for characters to embody it. I am not a novelist, but I suspect that no novelist has proceeded in that way ... That method may produce, or permit, admirable short stories in which, because of their brevity, the plot is more visible than the characters; but it cannot produce admirable novels, in which the overall form (if there is any) is only visible at the end and in which a single poorly imagined character may contaminate with unreality all those characters who surround him" ("Nathaniel Hawthorne," *Otras inquisiciones*).

So, then: distrust of the scale demanded by the novel and esteem for a format ("summary", "commentary") that makes "overall form" visible. As an expression of flexible disdain, of willingness to allow for occasional greatness in the practice of what he considers an erroneous genre, that phrase "if there is any" belongs to the same family as Valéry's most categorical observations. But the interesting thing about this apathy is that it does not suppose a rejection of narrative. In fact, a summary analysis of the most distinguishing characteristics in Borges's "fiction" reveals its undisguised narrative quality. The text may be a review of nonexistent literary works ("The Approach to Almotásim," "An Examination of the Works of Herbert Quain"), the exposition of apocryphal theories ("Three Versions of Judas," "The Theologians"), a report about an invented reality ("The Babylonian Lottery," "The Library of Babel"), even the connecting of probable episodes by means of a fictitious link ("History of the Warrior and the Captive," "Averroes' Search"). No matter. The less those texts respond to the accepted statutes of fiction, the more strongly they display the narrative process, which directs a mise-en-scène whose purpose is neither mimetic nor representational but intellectual: to arouse pleasure in the recognition of that "overall form," a recognition customarily postponed by the novel.

"The Wall and the Books," "Coleridge's Dream," "The Meeting in a Dream," and "The Modesty of History" are usually read as essays because they are included in a volume that announces itself as a collection of essays: *Otras inquisiciones*. The book's real nature is a series of narrative exercises, operations that renew the workings of narrative on philosophical ideas, historical documents, and literary figures. Similarly, "History of the Warrior and Captive" or "Averroes' Search" appear in *El Aleph* (The Aleph) and therefore are read as "fictions." Borges's categories of narrative do not discriminate between fiction and nonfiction. The only purpose of these categories is to exhibit the inherent qualities of narrative and essayistic discourse: to unearth a design that rescues the mere telling from chaos and makes an illusion of the cosmos possible. Fiction triumphs. Tlön captures and supplants the real universe with the illusion of order: "How can one not submit to Tlön, to the minute and vast evidence of an ordered planet? It is useless to answer that reality is also ordered. Perhaps it is, but in accordance with divine laws — I translate: with inhuman laws — that we never really perceive. Tlön will be a labyrinth, but a labyrinth planned by men, a labyrinth destined to be deciphered by men" ("Tlön, Uqbar, Orbis Tertius," *El jardín de senderos que si bifurcan*).

Looking back after twenty years, Borges pronounced judgement on his first stories: "They are the irresponsible game of a timid man who did not dare to write stories and so amused himself by falsifying and betraying (sometimes without aesthetic justification) other writers' stories" (Prologue to the 1954 edition of the *Historia universal de la infamia*). *To falsify, to betray* — those verbs shock with their criminal connotations. Yet they apply to the transmission of every story, from the traditional tale and gossip to any projected novel being transformed into a written text. All narrative proceeds by repetitions and modifications of a *pre*-text, which it nullifies. Those "ambiguous games" that Borges mentions in his prologue quoted above are especially revealing because they reject the invention of anecdote, choosing to explore, instead, the distinct possibilities of narrative, even the mutually exclusive possibilities. In order to overcome his declared timidity, Borges both disguises and exhibits his own devices.

How did Borges view those games at the time he wrote them? In his prologue to the first edition, Borges says: "They derived, I believe, from my re-reading of Stevenson and Chesterton, and even from the first films of von Sternberg, and perhaps from a certain biography of Evaristo Carriego. They abuse some procedures: random enumeration, abrupt shifts in continuity, reduction of a man's entire life to two or three scenes." This enumeration of sources and methods, by contrast, is not random. In fact, examining his examples enables us to define the context Borges discovered for his idea of film.

In Stevenson, even in Chesterton, Borges admires a capacity for verbal mise-en-scène:

"The threads of a story come from time to time together and make a picture in the web; the characters fall from time to time into some attitude to each other or to nature, which stamps the story home like an illustration. Crusoe recoiling from the foot-print, Achilles shouting over against the Trojans, Ulysses bend-ing the great bow, Christian running with his fingers in his ears, these are each culminating moments in the legend, and each has been printed on the mind's eye for ever. Other things we may forget; we may forget the words, athough they are beautiful; we may forget the author's comment although perhaps it was ingenious and true; but these epoch-making scenes, which put the last mark of truth upon a story and fill up, at one blow, our capacity for sympathetic pleasure, we so adopt into the very bosom of our mind that neither time nor tide can efface or weaken the impression. This, then, is the plastic part of litera-ture: to embody character, thought or emotion in some act or attitude that shall be remarkably striking to the mind's eye. (Stevenson, "A Gossip on Romance," *Memories and Portraits*, 1887)."

Appreciation of verbal mise-en-scène, which Stevenson calls "the plastic part of literature," appears at a particular point in the evolution of narrative during the second half of the nine-teenth century: after the inauguration of rigorous discipline by Flaubert; coincident with Henry James's early mastery in controlling points of view and alternating between "panorama" and "scene"; immediately before the consecration of these devices as technique in James's subsequent work as well as in the works of Conrad, Ford Maddox Ford, and the Joyce of "The Dead." Once systematized by Percy Lubbock in *The Craft of Fiction* and before languishing in the universities until it died out, this tradition provided the basis for the New Critics' best work in the study of fiction.

In "The Postulation of Reality," which appears in *Discusión* Borges refers to these verbal, defining, and definitive images as "circumstantial invention," the third and most difficult as well as efficient among the methods by which novelists can impose their subtle authority on the reader. He illustrates the method, magnanimously, with an example from *La gloria de Don Ramiro* and adds: "I have quoted a short, linear example, but I know of expanded works — Wells's rigorously imaginative novels, Defoe's exasperatingly true-to-life ones — that use no other technique than incorporating or serializing those laconic details into a lengthy development. I assert the same thing about Josef von Sternberg's cinematographic novels, which are also made up of significant moments. It is an admirable and difficult method, but its general application makes it less strictly literary than the two previous ones." (This quotation comes from the 1957 edition of *Discusión*; the original 1932 edition reads: "cinematic, ocular novels.")

What can a writer do with the novelist's tools if his own intellectual habits and work with language predispose him to writing short stories and brief, intense texts? If he is also intolerant of the novel's unavoidable long stretches? Instead of finding privileged moments in the course of narrating, is it possible for him to depart from an ordering of those "significant moments" and to omit the connective tissue that should bind them together? Or, going even further, will he be able with those isolated images — so memorable within a narrative of a certain length — to conjure up phantasmagorically the absent narration that is their "lengthy development"? *Evaristo Carriego* proposes an answer.

Comparable only to Nabokov's *Nikolai Gogol* as an example of the absorption of one literary figure by another (even though the minor stature of Carriego makes the process more apparent), Borges's 1930 biography of Carriego — with its discreet "betraying" and "falsifying" of another's story that scarcely serves as a pretext — is also his first approach toward that "fiction" from which a particular timidity had held him back. At several points, Borges declares his hesitations, the obstacles he encounters in writing the book. In the first chapter — "The Palermo Section of Buenos Aires" — one reads: "The jumbled, incessant style of reality, with its punctuation of ironies, surprises, and intimations as strange as surprises, could only be recaptured by a novel, which would be out of place here." And how can he represent Palermo as it was before he knew it?

To recapture that almost static prehistory would be to foolishly weave a chronicle of infinitesimal processes.... The most direct means, according to cinematographic procedure, would be to propose a continuity of discontinuous images: a yoke of wine-bearing mules, the wild ones with their eyes blindfolded; a long, still expanse of water with willow leaves floating on the surface; a vertiginous, poor lost soul, wading through the flooding streams on stilts; the open countryside, with nothing to do; the tracks of a hacienda's stubbornly trampled cattle path, the route to corrals in the north; a peasant (against the dawn sky) who dismounts and slits his jaded horse's wide throat; a wisp of smoke wafting through the air.

A relationship is established among these images. In "A Gossip on Romance" Stevenson had expounded his observations as a reader and sought support from them for his method as a writer. Borges, who agrees with those observations, sees them as applicable to the films of von Sternberg; and in his early *Evaristo Carriego*, where he doubts the very fiction whose elements he invokes, he attempts the magic of conjuring up a more abundant, unlimited reality by naming some notable moments that may postulate it. Film suggests to him the possibility of connecting those moments by means of a less discursive syntax than the verbal. Here a notion that might be termed *montage* appears, operating in texts made from words. That "cinematographic procedure," that "continuity of discontinuous images" will be the stated method in the stories of *Historia universal de la infamia*. One of the chapters that divide — and integrate — "The Disinterested Killer Bill Harrigan" opens: "History (which like a certain director, proceeds by discontinuous images) now proposes the image of a ..."

The stories in *Historia universal de la infamia* illustrate, point by point, Chesterton's observations in his study of Stevenson: "Those flat figures could only be seen from one side. They are aspects or attitudes of men rather than men" (*R. L. Stevenson*, London, 1928). The stories also illustrate what Chesterton noted about "our modern attraction to short stories" and the "short story today" in his study of Dickens: "We get a glimpse of grey streets of London, or red plains of India, as in an opium vision; we see people, arresting people with fiery and appealing faces. But when the story is ended, the people are ended" (*Charles Dickens*, London, 1906). To the degree that they ignore what Chesterton in his book on Stevenson calls "huge hospitality for their own characters" and, like Stevenson, prefer a certain thinness in characterization, a simplification appropriate to marionette theater, the two-dimensionality of colored illustrations, Borges's early fictional essays stage a narrative mechanism more than any particular narrative itself. And they do so with the clear awareness that the mechanism is identical in written and cinematographic fiction. (A connection can be seen between this procedure and *Nabakov's Dozen*, in which the destinies of various Russian adventurers, exiled in Berlin during the 1920's and linked occasionally to movies as extras, are recapitulated in takes, sequences, lighting effects, and montage in order to establish a parodic intent.)

There was a moment, which might be situated between *Evaristo Carriego* and the writing of his first story, "Man on the Rose-colored Corner," when Stevenson and von Sternberg equally aroused Borges's attention, a moment when it seemed possible to submit Palermo's turn-of-the-century toughs as well as the neighborhood itself to a verbal treatment, the equivalent of von Sternberg's treatment of Chicago and its gangsters in *Underworld*. Impatient with the restraints that the novel seemed to impose on the exercise of fiction, Borges attempted fiction by cultivating a lucid magic. It matters little whether he was guided by the possibilities revealed to him in narratives by his favorite writers or if their writings permitted him to observe these possibilities in films.

Continuity and *discontinuity*: cinematographic language provided the point of departure for Borges's play with these concepts in his first attempts at fiction.

All narrative traditionally works by successive effects of continuity, with suspense deriving from an apparently defective continuity later restored by an intermediate connection. Poetry, on the other hand, traditionally orders its emphases spatially, ignoring all requirements for connective relation other than the formal. Enumeration is one such relation, and Borges had cultivated it in his early fiction, obviously pleased with organizing his prose in a form unprecedented by the nineteenth-century novel. Every rhetorical work in the enumerative form invokes the supposed "endless variety of creation" by alluding to that creation with incongrous signs — a procedure whose illustrious, theological, and pantheistic genealogy cannot be reduced to Spitzer's "chaotic enumeration," which is linked to one notion of modernity. Nevertheless, a single characteristic is invariable: enumeration is always the double operation of naming in order to indicate the unnamed, of making the spaces between signs as denotative as the markers measuring their extension. Enumeration proposes to express the inexpressible; and, although it relies on only one scheme — enumeration — it is, like storytelling itself, syntactic by nature.

In enumeration, the discontinuity of the actual text seems to be endowed with the prestige of representing an absent, still greater text. Similarly, in *Discusión* and *Otras inquisiciones*, Borges suggests that far from denying the figure of Whitman, all the information about the poet's persona scattered throughout Whitman's work confirms his mythic stature. A comparable mechanism controls the lists of irreconciliable or merely dissimilar unities that dizzyingly sketch the infinite in such stories as "The Aleph," "The Zahir," "The Writing of the Gods," and even in the comparatively brief list of incarnations in "The Immortal."

By 1935, Borges's enumerations in *Historia universal de la infamia* reveal how they function as concealed illusionism: they display properties of narrative usually disguised in the very act of being employed. The most famous example is the list of effects brought about by the fickle piety of Fra Bartolome de las Casas in "The Terrible Redeemer Lazarus Morell." The terms in these enumerations — or the arguments united in a discourse — appear separated by what really connects them, as if by an electrical current: incongruity, paradox, simple alternation. At the same time, the enumerative combination as a whole registers the ironic richness of these minor clashes. Without the circuitry of conflict and ellipsis, these separate elements would lapse into the inertia of a historic or fictitious report uncharged by narrative.

It is no accident that, beginning with its title, an early Borges essay joins "narrative art" and "magic." His first fictions perform a kind of illusion: that *post hoc, ergo propter hoc*, an error in logic whose systematic cultivation, for Barthes, is the narrative operation par excellence, "the language of Fate." (Valéry also considered that associating the novelistic or even the fantastic world with reality was of the same order as associating *trompe l'oeil* with the tangible objects among which the viewer moves.) And what is that language of Fate if not an idea of montage? Cinematographic or verbal montage, which, in the chaotic archive of humanity's acts, proposes or discovers a meaning by ordering those "culminating moments" and "major scenes" in which Stevenson saw the proof and effect of the highest fiction? Stevenson saw it as operating on different levels of fiction and nonfiction, of history and fantasy. Its name, quite simply, is narrative.

Translated by Gloria Waldman and Ronald Christ

Borges on Film
Jorge Luis Borges

Q: I know that you've written some film criticism.

Jorge Luis Borges: Oh yes, I'm very fond of films. Of course, in Buenos Aires, people go to far more films than they do here [the U.S.]. In Buenos Aires every day, well I suppose you can choose between forty different films, and those films, well most of them are American, but you can also have your pick of Swedish, English, French and Italian films, or even Russian films.*

As Edgardo Cozarinsky demonstrated in the preceding article, the young Borges was greatly influenced by the cinema. During the 1930s and 40s, he wrote many film reviews for the Argentine literary journal Sur. *These are reproduced in Cozarinsky's forthcoming book* Borges in/and/on Film. *Here we have reproduced most of the - lamentably few - reviews Borges wrote of Argentine films during this period, and those reviews that, in their discussion of American cinema, touch on debates in Argentine literary circles concerning national culture.*

Few attempts have been made to adapt Borges' writing to film; perhaps because, although Edgardo Cozarinsky argues eir essentially "cinematic" qualities, they do not lend themselves to standard film narrative techniques.

Jorge Luis Borges died in June 1986 in Geneva, Switzerland, where he had recently resettled.

---

* "Jorge Luis Borges Interviewed by Richard Burgin," from *Behind the Scenes: Theater and Film Interviews from The Transatlantic Review*, Joseph F. McCrindle ed., Holt, Rinehart and Winston, New York 1971.

1. La fuga

To enter a moviehouse on Lavalle Street in Buenos Aires and find myself (not without surprise) on the Gulf of Bengal or on Wabash Avenue seems preferable to entering that same moviehouse and finding myself (not without surprise) on Lavalle Street. I make this preliminary confession so that no one will attribute my defense of an Argentine film to murky feelings of patriotism. To idolize a ridiculous scarecrow because it is autochthonous, to fall asleep for the fatherland, to take pleasure in tedium because it is a national product — all seem absurd to me.

The primary virtue that may be distinguished in *La fuga* (The Flight) is continuity. There are numerous films that never go beyond mere photographic anthologies — *La passion de Jeanne d'Arc* (The Passion of Joan of Arc) continues to be the mirror and archetype of this much praised error — and perhaps there is not a single European film that does not suffer from fruitless images. In contrast, *La fuga* flows limpidly, the way American films do. Buenos Aires, but Saslavsky spares us the *Congreso,* the *Puerto de Riachuelo*, the *Obeliski*, a ranch in the state of Entre Rios, but Saslavsky spares us the breaking in of horses, the branding of cattle, the two-horse 100 meter dash, the dueling guitars, and the all too predictably shrewd *gauchos* who boss around authentic Italians.

The second virtue: the director has ignored the plot's tendency to tear-jerking. His villains practice murder the way someone practices a profession: they do not yearn for their native hut in elegaic tangos, and they are ruled by a serious German gentleman who delights in stuffed animals and lives in a functional house, thanks to the example of Gropius. It is true that one of the heroines gives up her life for her man, but it is just as true that she does not remain sexually faithful to him, as a North American director would have demanded. A detective helps her. This man (the surest and most admirable of touches) is much friendlier than the villains he chases.

The scene of the woman's death — the scene of her inaudible, dying voice — is the film's most intense. Another high point is the girl's astonishing joy on learning that two years — only two years — separate her from a joy she thought close at hand.

As for the defects ... I realize that with good logic we can reduce them to one: the slow-footed, painful comedy. *Mutatis mutandis*, the plot of *La fuga* is that of Chaplin's famous film, *The Preacher*, badly rebaptized in Latin America as *El reverendo caradura* (The Shameless Preacher).* I do not disapprove of annexing this plot; I do disapprove of the ingenuous supposition that there are many grotesque possibilities left to explore in a story that has already been used by Chaplin. The ones *La fuga* proposes to us — the young man who sits down on flypaper, the young man who holds a conversation with no pants on — are very awkward. Another, perhaps irreparable mistake: the insertion of farcical characters (in this case the Principal of the little school) who contaminate the others with unreality. The others, and the story that houses them.
— *SUR*, No. 36, August 1937

La fuga. Argentina, 1937. 92 minutes. Director: Luis Saslavsky. Screenplay: Alfredo G. Volpe. Photography: John Alton. Cast: Santiago Arrieta, Tita Merello, Francisco Petrone, Niní Gambier. A *Pampa Film* production.

La passion de. Jeanne d'Arc. France, 1927. 110 minutes, cut to 86. Director: Carl Dreyer. Screenplay: Carl Dreyer, Joseph Delteil, based on the original records of the trial. Photography: Rudolph Maté. Cast: Maria Falconetti, Eugène Silvain, Maurice Schutz, Michel Simon, Antonin Artaud. A *Sociéte Générale de Films* production.

The Pilgrim. U.S.A., 1923. 4 reels. Direction and screenplay: Charles Chaplin. Associate director: Chuck Riesner. Photography: Rollie Totheroh. Cast: Charles Chaplin, Edna Purviance, Kitty Bradbury, Mack Swain, Loyal Underwood. A First National Films production.

* Borges is evidently thinking of *The Pilgrim*. [E.C.]

2. Green Pastures

Let us imagine a translation of the Bible to the time and space —
conventional — of *gaucho* literature. (It is impossible that someone has not already yielded to the temptation of trying it.)
In this reduction, the Devil is Mandinga, God is Daddy Dios,
Abel is a rancher murdered by the farmer Cain, Pontius Pilate
is the Commanding Officer, the Virgin Mary interrupts her
hymn to the Holy Trinity in order to respond: "Conceived
without sin" to the "Hail Mary, full of grace" of a dusty, early-
rising Angel, who has not even gotten off his wolf-gray horse.
It is pointless to reveal other touches no less predictable and
cumbersome: my readers can already get a foretaste of the
special horror of this wild, Biblical hodge-podge. I want them
to imagine it, and to detest it, so that I then may declare:
That, precisely, is what *Green Pastures* is not.

To deny that identity is not to pretend that the bituminous
Dead Sea — and Paradise — differ less from Louisiana or Georgia
than from the Province of Buenos Aires. My thesis is different.
I think that to appropriate the men of scripture or the men of
Eduardo Gutiérrez* bothers us for the simple reason that it is
an arbitrary procedure. (Which, let it be said between parentheses,
is the annoying original sin of our creole *Faust* — its joining of
the 16th century to the 19th, of Saxony to Bragado, is totally
haphazard).† Not so Connelly's *Green Pastures*. The author
states that "*Green Pastures* is an attempt to present certain
aspects of a living religion in the terms of its believers. The
religion is that of thousands of Negroes in the deep South. With
terrific spiritual hunger and the greatest humility these untutored
black Christians — many of whom cannot even read the book

---

* Eduardo Gutiérrez (1853-1890) was an Argentine author of numerous
  gauchesque novels in the serial or *folletín* manner. [Trans.]
† *Fausto*, a gauchesque poem published in 1870 by the Argentine poet
  Estanislao de Campo (1834-1880). In pointedly picturesque language,
  the poem gives the impression of one of the gauchos who has attended
  a performance of Gundos' *Faust*. [Trans.]
** Marc Connelly, *The Green Pastures*, New York, 1929, p. 55. Borges's
  translation conforms substantially to the opening paragraph of the
  "Author's Note," quoted here. [Trans.]

which is the treasure house of their faith — have adapted the contents of the Bible to the consistencies of their everyday lives."** The numerous anachronisms (and anatropisms) that the adjustment gives rise to certainly do not exhaust the film's charms. We are amused when God saves the 10¢ cigar, which the Archangel has just offered him, "for later"; we are amused when rheumatic pains warn Noah of the approaching flood; we are amused when God, walking through the fields, asks some flowers how they are, and they answer him in unison, with a piping, child-like voice: "We O.K., Lawd."

People will tell me that the foregoing is ingenuous. I reply: yes, just as ingenuous as that "Lord God walking in the garden in the cool of the day" (Genesis, III:8). Do I dare add that I prefer the idea of a human God, an awkward God, a God capable of repenting, to the idea proposed by the theologians of a happily verbal monster, made up of three inextricable Persons and nineteen attributes? To the idea of a God about whom Wells said that he cannot act because he is all-powerful and eternal, cannot think because he is omniscient, cannot move because he is ubiquitous and is already everywhere.
— *SUR*, No. 37, October 1937

Green Pastures, U.S.A., 1936. 10 reels. Directors: Marc Connelly, William Keighley. Screenplay based on the fable in dialogue by Marc Connelly, suggested by *Ol' Man Adam an' His Chillun*, Southern tales by Roark Bradford. Photography: Al Mohr. Cast: Rex Ingram, Eddie Anderson, Oscar Polk. A Warner Bros. picture.

3. The Road Back

In the winter of 1872, among the *jacaranda* furniture of a hotel whose balconies faced the treeless Plaza de la Victoria, Don José Hernández — enemy of Sarmiento and of Mitre — wanted to expose the degradation that the disastrous military regime had produced in the natives of Buenos Aires and wrote the anti-war poem *Martín Fierro*. The hero — who doesn't know it? — was a deserter from the army; his companion a deserter from the police. We are familiar with the consequences. Around 1894,

Unamuno discovered that Hernández's book "was the song of the Spanish fighter who, after having planted the cross in Granada, went to America to serve the progress of civilization and to open the road into the desert." In 1916, Lugones stated, "and for that reason — because it personifies the heroic life of the people with their language and their most genuine feelings, embodying it in a champion or, rather, in the most perfect emblem of justice and liberation — *Martín Fierro* is an epic poem."

I have recalled the instance of *Martín Fierro* because it is not unusual. Works denouncing the indignities or the horrors of war always run the risk of seeming to be a vindication of war. In fact, the more horrible the war, the greater its satanic prestige, the greater the virtue of those men who look it in the face. That obstinate Dr. Johnson, who once declared that "Patriotism is the last refuge of a scoundrel," also said, around 1778, "The profession of soldiers and sailors has the dignity of danger." What remains in our memory, right now, of the acclaimed pacifist film *All Quiet on the Western Front*? A fierce and enviable bayonet charge, exactly like the ones shown in any war movie.

The Road Back is undeniably inferior to *All Quiet on the Western Front*. Its climactic moment is also a battle. The peculiar pathos of the scene comes from its being absolutely clear to us that the soldiers' fears and agonies are futile: Germany had already surrendered. The other scenes, it seems to me, are entirely forgettable. The thesis (I think) is the unadaptability of soldiers to civilian life, the conflict between the ethic of the city and the ethic of the trench. Fear of rendering the protagonists disagreeable has dulled — or invalidated — the demonstration of this thesis. It is true that one of the veterans ends up a murderer, but his victim is such an execrable, such an oily, such a minutely Jewish *Schieber* that his destruction is a worthy act in any light. Another of the veteran fighters ends up in a marriage of convenience, another improvising speeches, another coveting (and stealing) other people's chickens.

On seeing *The Road Back* I felt that mere pacifism is not enough. War is an ancient passion that tempts men with ascetic and mortal charms. In order to abolish it, you have to confront it with another passion. Maybe that of the *good European*

— Leibniz, Voltaire, Goethe, Arnold, Renan, Shaw, Russell, Unamuno, T.S. Eliot — who recognizes himself as the heir and the perpetuator of all countries. Unfortunately, Europe is teeming with mere Germans and mere Irishmen. Europeans are scarce.
— *SUR*, No. 38, November 1937

The Road Back. U.S.A., 1937. 12 reels. Director: James Whale. Screenplay: R.C. Sherriff, Charles Kenyon. Based on the novel by Erich Maria Remarque. Photography: John Mescall. Cast: John King, Richard Cromwell, "Slim" Summerville, Andy Devine, Louise Fazenda. Associate Producer: Edmund Grainger. A Universal picture.

All Quiet On The Western Front. U.S.A., 1930. 140 minutes. Director: Lewis Milestone. Screenplay: Del Andrews, Maxwell Anderson, George Abbott, with dialogue by Anderson and Abbott. Based on the novel by Erich Maria Remarque. Photography: Arthur Edeson. Cast: Lewis Ayres, Louis Wolheim, John Wray, George "Slim" Summerville, Russell Gleason. Producer: Carl Laemmle, Jr. A Universal picture.

4. Prisioneros de la tierra

Two characters join their futile forces to make *Prisioneros de la tierra* (Prisoners of the Earth) intolerable, unwatchable. One: the huge and staggering Dr. Else, an unrecognized precursor of *ultraismo** ("The red earth imprisons men..."; "I have been wrapped in a moist sudatorium for twenty-five years..") who parades his face — an enormous lion's or king's, straight off a playing card — from one end of the film to the other and succeeds in being no less overwhelming than the frightful Emil Jannings. The other: a certain amateur encyclopedist who shakes his mutilated arm with joyful persistence and repeats

* A literary movement that Borges introduced to Argentina on his return from Europe in 1921. It was characterized by an attempt to reduce poetry to paratactic images and metaphors. Borges later repudiated this phase of his literary career. [Trans.]

over and over: "I am a happy man. What more do I need to be happy?" Or, "Don't you know that to love is to understand?"

In spite of these "conversationists," the film is good, even very good. It is superior — faint praise! — to many that our resigned republic has given birth to (and applauded). It is also superior to most of the films that California and Paris have sent us recently. One incredible and sure touch: there is not a single comic scene in the course of this exemplary film. To ignore Sandrini, to successfully elude Pepe Arias, and to avert Catita are three forms of happiness our directors have not entered upon before now.* Clearly, these negative merits are not the only ones.

There is a powerful plot, uncontaminated by either virginal North American tawdriness (in the first scene, the protagonist walks out of a brothel) or by that other neo-tawdriness, which in every French film gives us a fleeting, epigrammatic glimpse of a pair of lovers. There is a character — the vicious Koerner (with his core of unviolated loneliness, his Beethoven record, and his resigning himself to being cruel and hated), who certainly is more lifelike than the hero. I have been — which of my friends doesn't know it? — an insatiable and fervent patron of Milton Sills, of Kohler, and of Bancroft;† I do not recall, in such a bloody picture, a more powerful scene than the next-to-last in *Prisioneros de la tierra*, where the man is horsewhipped into a final river. That man is brave, that man is arrogant, that man is taller than the other ... In similar scenes in other pictures, brutal people are appointed to perform brutal actions; in *Prisioneros de la tierra* the hero is appointed, and he is almost intolerably efficient. (If I am not mistaken, this wonderful assignment is the handiwork of Ulysses Petit de Murat; the two actors perform the scene very well.)

---

* The top three comic actors in Argentine cinema in the 1930s and '40s. [ed.]

† Three leading men of Hollywood: Milton Sills (1882-1930) starred in many silent movies such as *The Claw* (1917) and *The Sea Wolf* (1930); Fred Kohler (1889-1938) specialized as a villain in Westerns such as *The Iron Horse* (1924); and George Bancroft played toughs and villains in movies like *Docks of New York* (1928) and *Scandal Sheet* (1931). Both Kohler and Bancroft appeared in von Sternberg's *Underworld*. [Trans.]

Another memorable moment occurs when, from his horse, one of the *mate* plantation owners kills the half-enslaved peon with a single, laconic bullet and does not even turn his head to see his victim fall; still another: the woman's passionate flight through the tremulous mountain night.

Photography, admirable.

— *SUR*, No. 60, September 1939

Prisioneros de la tierra. Argentina, 1939. 85 minutes. Director: Mario Soffici. Screenplay: Darío Quiroga, Ulysses Petit de Murat. Based on stories by Horacio Quiroga. Photography: Pablo Tabernero. Cast: Francisco Petrone, Angel Magaña, Roberto Fugazot, Homero Carpena, Elisa Galvé. A *Pampa Film* production.

Translated by Gloria Waldman and Ronald Christ

Report on the State of Argentine Cinema
Sindicato de la Industria Cinematográfica Argentina

This report was presented by Jorge Ventura, the Secretary General of SICA, the Argentine film workers' union, to the first-ever conference of Latin American film workers' unions at the seventh Festival of New Latin American Cinema, held in Havana, Cuba, in December 1985. The report credits its sources as the book El síndrome del cine nacional *by Jaime Lozano (1985), the Argentine film magazine* Heraldo del cine *and* SICA's *own files.*

SICA comprises and represents film workers in any capacity. It is affiliated with the *CGT (Confderación General de Trabajadores)*, the only national trade union in Argentina. Those working in the production of commercials, documentaries, shorts and feature films are legally entitled to join the union, the only one recognized throughout the country. Its members include the so-called transitory workers, technicians whose workload depends on the duration of filming and pre- and post-production, as well as permanent employees and film and sound lab technicians.

SICA is almost a half-century old. Its influence was at first weak and sporadic, as it joined solitary activists in fighting for just salaries and working conditions. It is worth remembering that in the 1930s and into the 1940s shooting days in Argentina were often eighteen hours long, and it was common to see workers sleeping in the studios in order to cope with such intense working days. Often, technicians would work on one film in the morning and another in the afternoon.

The enormous popularity of film in those days led to the growth of a work force of 5,000 technicians working in the medium. Production at this time averaged forty-two feature films per year, in a country of 15 million inhabitants.

Nevertheless, the interruption of a popular political process, the instability of the industry, and the actions of foreign monopolies, with the complicity of the national liberal oligarchy, brought about the progressive erosion of our film industry and introduced a succession of periodic crises which have debilitated it.

Only twelve feature films were produced in 1983, the last year of the military dictatorship. This was the smallest number of films produced in many years. The population of Argentina was then thirty million inhabitants. During that year there was a veritable invasion of foreign films, 42% of which were North American. The active work force in the Argentine film industry was reduced to 1,200 people. Film labs laid off more than 50% of their personnel; in one case the dismissals accounted for 75% of the workers. Wages dropped, health and safety regulations were not observed, and the Collective Agreement was systematically violated.

From all this it is easy to note the consequences of this process of de-nationalization:

1. Lack of work;
2. Cultural and ideological penetration, with all the dangers this implies, including demoralization and lack of pride in our own work;
3. Subjection of a cultural medium to the goals of multinationals striving to sell their goods;
4. A de-culturation process that turns us into spectators and consumers of life, instead of being its protagonists.

Film Under Democracy

The Constitutional Government that has been ruling Argentina for the past two years has taken some positive steps to protect citizens' rights and powers, in order to establish a basis for democratic development. This, in our judgement, must be complemented by economic measures that protect our industry and culture. This would allow for the development of a more just society, bringing us closer to our Latin American roots, the dream and necessity of our present epoch.

During this time film censorship has been abolished and a system has been implemented that protects minors while freeing the adult spectators from the protectors of his or her consciousness. The *Instituto Nacional de Cinematografía* has been returned to the control of film people* and a 10% tax on film admissions has been reintroduced for use by *INC*. In 1984, twenty-six feature films were made.

By August of 1985, only fifteen films had been made; a result, in our minds, of the persistence of the control of the local market by the large film multi-nationals in alliance with their national representatives. The reluctance to intervene against this structure has produced inequalities that have forced independent national producers to limit production.

This problem has been aggravated in the past year by the argument of some larger producers (who are also distributors of foreign films) — an argument that has a certain amount of official support — that the problem of Argentine cinema is to be found in the production process. An attempt is being made on the basis of this argument to lower wages in the production sector and alter contract agreements. Without denying the possibility of rationalizing our production sector further, the country's film technicians, with the support of actors, directors and some independent producers, have vigorously countered this argument. A compromise has resulted, and *INC* has now undertaken to focus its efforts on the area of distribution and exhibition. A program of state production credits has subsequently acted as an incentive to small independent producers, who have put new films into production, which leads us to believe that by the end of the year we will approach 1984's output.†

The present state of the Argentine film industry is characterized by the following:

Production
1. Full thematic freedom exists.
2. State production credits, which mostly benefit small inde-

* *INC* was under direct military administration under the Junta. [ed.]
† Depending on how one calculates annual production (by completion or release date), 1985's production was almost exactly the same as the figure given here for production in 1984. [ed.]

pendent directors/producers, have been implemented.*
3. The possibility exists for producers to receive advance payments from distributors to defray the cost of the final processing of the film.
4. Some technicians, actors and directors are willing to defer their salaries in order to keep a film in production. This situation sometimes leads to the total loss of their wages due.
5. Large producers with their own equipment are few — only one has sound studios — and the themes they usually adapt are those that present the least commercial risk, those of the most passive kind.

The average cost of a film is approximately $280,000 U.S., of which 22% is paid to a technical team averaging 28 people. The average length of production, including shooting and pre- and post-production, is seven weeks.

Distribution

There are three types of film distributors in Argentina:
1. Those that distribute mostly Argentine and some foreign films.
2. National distributors that distribute exclusively foreign films.
3. Subsidiaries of U.S. companies that distribute their own films.

Argentine distributors who buy films on the international market, mostly European films, are subjected to a "package" buying system. The packages contain a fixed number of films, containing only one or two films of interest and seven or eight films with little or no commercial or artistic value. In this way, fill-in material must be screened in order to recoup costs, further limiting the access of national films to the country's movie screens. This trash also contributes to a debasement of taste and represents an unnecessary drain of foreign exchange. Neither the Argentine distributors of foreign films nor the U.S. subsidiaries reinvest a single dollar of their huge profits in national film production, because there is no obligation for them to do so.

---

* No discrimination is made in awarding the credits however, and Argentina's largest and most successful production houses benefit from them as well. [ed.]

Some 4,400 foreign films have played in the Argentine market in the past fifteen years, averaging 293 per annum. The maximum number was reached in 1970, when 391 foreign films were screened, and the minimum was in 1975 with 204. Between 40 and 50% of these foreign films were imported from the U.S. by members of *La Camara Argentino-Norteamericano de Distribuidores de Films* (The Argentine-North American Chamber of Film Distributors / The Film Board), affiliated with the Motion Picture Association of America (MPAA), which groups together U.S. producers. The main members of the Film Board are the CIC (Cinema International Corporation, a merger of Paramount Universal, Metro Goldwyn Mayer and United Artists in 1982), Columbia, Fox, and Warner. The last three operate from the same building. All these firms form the great monopoly of world film distribution and are linked to huge trans-national corporations. The CIC, for example, has links with RCA, Pepsi Cola, the Hilton Hotels chain, and the owners of General Dynamics (builders of the fighter bomber Delta F-106). Metro Goldwyn Mayer has links with the Time-Life group and with Time-Life films. Warner Bros. belongs to the Kinner National Service Corporation (banks, insurance and communications); Columbia Pictures was acquired by Coca Cola in 1983; together with banks, airlines and building firms, United Artists comprises the Transamerica Corporation; and Paramount is part of Gulf Western Industries (insurance companies, tobacco, raw materials, etc.).

All these firms are thus linked to those firms that help determine the protectionist policies of the U.S., expressed through measures such as dumping, overpricing of products, overvaluation of the dollar, arbitrary and excessive interest rates, and the decline in prices paid for raw materials coming from the so-called Third World, of which all of Latin America is a part. In a word, these companies represent the cream of the creditors of our foreign debt.

The local firms which comprise the *Asociación Argentina de Distribuidores de Películas* (The Argentine Association of Film Distributors) distribute the rest of the foreign films brought into Argentina. There are about ten firms of varying importance in this group.

Finally, distributors of Argentine films are grouped into two organizations: *La Asociación de Productores* (The General Association of Producers) and *El Centro de Distribuidores de Películas Argentinas (CDPA* — The Argentine Film Distribution Centre). The first is composed of organizations such as *Argentina Sono Film, Victoria Cinematográfica* and *Aries Cinematográfica.* Over the past two years it has been possible to detect a marked increase in the number of foreign films distributed by these companies, as well as in the number of co-productions with U.S. companies they undertake. In the case of *Aries*, for example, five films have been made in co-production with Roger Corman and eight foreign films were distributed in 1984, rising to eighteen in 1985.

These companies began as film producers that later began to distribute their own films to ensure their exhibition. They have since been sought out by smaller independent producers to distribute their films. One can only expect this trend to progress in the future, leading to a relatively monopolistic situation.

To complete this brief sketch, 157 films were released in the first half of 1985. Only eleven of these were Argentine, and 75% of the remaining 146 were from the U.S. and the European Economic community, countries with whom Argentina has the greatest foreign debt.* Of this total only six films were Brazilian and none were from other Latin American countries, Africa or Asia.

Last year, Argentine films accounted for 8.5% of the nation's screen-time and produced 18.7% of the spectators, or approximately ten million out of a total fifty-five million spectators.

Exhibition

There are now 1,117 movie theatres in Argentina. In 1967, the total was 2,200: in less than twenty years, the total number of cinemas has been reduced by nearly 50%. This illustrates the crisis affecting our industry. In most cases, the cinemas which have closed were in small provincial capitals, and their owners generally did not belong to any large circuit in the country. Most importantly, some of these cinemas were the only ones operating in certain towns in the interior of the country.

There are several reasons for this decline. The high per capita ownership of television in Argentina is just one of them. The

* Argentina's foreign debt now stands at $55 billion U.S. [ed.]

lack of adequate protection of Argentine cinema in its own market; the sustained and growing invasion of foreign films; the increase in illiteracy in the interior of the country; rising unemployment and a decline in salaries; the increase in admission prices (peaking at the equivalent of $5.10 U.S. in 1982; today it is $1.40); the thematic impoverishment of the national cinema; the changes in taste brought on by the systematic alienation and depersonalization of television — these are the main reasons for the decline of our cinema.

Added to these is the problem of home video — in Buenos Aires alone 35,000 titles a month are being rented. A sociological phenomenon previously unseen in our country is now taking place. People are moving away from public entertainment, avoiding social contact and confining themselves to the solitude of home entertainment. In this way, cultural products are consumed without the opportunity of formulating a collective critical attitude.

Of all the sectors of the film industry, exhibition is the strongest because it recoups 50% of the net revenue of a film. In this sector, there are two dominant circuits: *La Sociedad Anónima Argentina (SAC)* and the chain *Coll-Di Fiore-Saragusti*, which has recently taken over the *Lococo* chain. These Buenos Aires-based companies also control the most important theatres in the provinces. Their main source of income is the box office percentage, in addition to the sale of advertising space in cinemas and the revenue from commercial trailers in the programs.

These monopolistic firms are the least likely to support measures to strengthen the Argentine film industry because their exclusive concern is profitability. Ninety percent of the material they show is foreign and they consistently reject Argentine films. It is also impossible to know if the number of patrons they declare really corresponds to the number of tickets sold.*

* A reference to suspicions that some exhibitors were under-reporting their ticket sales in order to profit from the 10% admission tax collected on behalf of the film institute. To counter this, *INC* has introduced a monthly raffle (with large cash prizes), drawn from ticket stubs film patrons bring to the film institute, thereby discouraging exhibitor fraud. [ed.]

SICA

As we stated in the introduction to this report, the union represents the film workers and expresses their points of view. Our action is based on general labour legislation and the Collective Agreement in force in the industry since 1975. We have also taken part in the fight to strengthen the national cinema, transcending the limits imposed on us by the prevailing system. Thus, along with the *Asociación Argentina de Actores* (Argentina Actors' Association), *Directores Argentinos Cinematográficos* (Argentine Film Directors) and *Argentores, SICA* co-founded the *Comité Permanente de Defensa del Cine Argentino* (Argentine Cinema Defence Group), an organization founded in 1968 to fight against censorship and blacklisting.

The military Junta also took from our ranks our share of victims of the aberration to which this country was subjected. Some of us were exiled or have "disappeared," but we have been able to reappear to fight with renewed vigor in the fight that we know is that of all of Latin America. During the Junta, we lost our personal and professional contacts, dangerous generation gaps appeared, and there was an attempt to suppress all aspects of our Argentine character. In a word, we were being prepared to meekly accept our subjugated role as consumers of cultural goods imposed on us by others. Because of all this, we began to develop, during our first year of activity in 1985*, professional development courses for our members and for students.

In exchanges with other countries, we have been able to benefit from the insights of people like Nikita Mijailkov, Antonio Bardem, Tomás Guitiérrez Alea, and Fernando Birri, who prepared a seminar on New Latin American Cinema for us.

Our present activities have the following objectives:

1. To defend the rights of the film workers of Argentina.
2. To increase the professional capacity of our members, through exchange visits by technicians, particularly within Latin America.
3. To strive for the elimination of the conditions that have paralysed our industry, linked to the fight in Latin America against ideological penetration and deculturization.
4. To establish professional alliances, through the *Comité*

---

* *SICA*'s activities were suspended under the Junta. [ed.]

Permanente de Defensa del Cine Argentino, with all those suffering the problems of ideological and economic domination by the film multi-nationals.

5. To structure a film law that responds to the true needs of the national industry. We have already drafted a blueprint for consideration by Congress.

6. To extract all that is possible from the existing law. The *Instituto Nacional de Cinematografía* is mandated to do this and it must exercise this mandate.

7. To implement a system that would provide Argentine cinema better access to its own market.

8. To prevent the infiltration of foreign made dupes, which destroys sources of work for Argentine technicians.

9. To legislate the compulsory exhibition of the Argentine short film.

A Latin American cinema will develop not only through our individual efforts, but by co-operation. For that reason, we support co-productions between our countries.

Foreign debt and cultural penetration go hand in hand toward a single objective: the subjection of our people to the dictates of those who view life as a marketplace for their products.

Translated by Alex Zisman

SICA *march in 1982, calling for the return of "missing" film workers.*

Chronology of Argentine Cinema
Tim Barnard

The following chronology of the development of Argentine cinema is of necessity skeletal and selective. The work of Domingo di Núbila (1960), Jorge Miguel Couselo (1984) and Octavio Getino (1978) were the major sources of information. However, material was selected here and there from virtually every source in the bibliography, so that errors of fact, omission, or interpretation remain the responsibility of the present author and should not reflect on the quality of work of the above historians.

1896   Less than one year after cinema's first appearance in a Paris café, the first Lumière films are exhibited in Buenos Aires.

1897   *La bandera argentina* (The Argentine Flag), by French immigrant Eugenio Py, is the first film shot in Argentina. It is 17 metres long.

1908   *El fusilamiento de Dorrego* (Dorrego's Execution) is made by the Italian immigrant Mario Gallo. Based on an event in Argentine history, it is Argentina's first dramatic short — previous production has been limited to newsreels and documentaries.

1909   Argentina's first labs and studios are built.

1914   Enrique García Velloso films *Amalia*, Argentina's first feature length dramatic film, based on a popular national literary classic by José Mármol.

1915 Eduardo Martínez de la Pera, Ernesto Gunch, and Humberto Cairo film *Nobleza gaucha* (Gaucho Nobility). It becomes the most popular Argentine — and Latin American — film of the silent period, and opens foreign markets to Argentine films for the first time. On an investment of 20,000 pesos, it returns 600,000 pesos to its producers. As its title suggests, its theme is entirely Argentine; its intertitles are taken from José Fernández's gaucho literary classic *Martín Fierro*.

During the First World War, Argentina establishes itself as an important exporter of films to the Hispanic market, benefitting from reduced production in Europe and the stimulating effect of *Nobleza gaucha*.

1917 A number of important national films are made. José Augustin Ferreyra films *La tango de la muerte* (Death's Tango), which shows the quotidian reality of working class life in Buenos Aires. Federico Valle produces and Quirino Cristiani, Diógenes Taborda, and Andrés Decaud direct *El apóstol* (The Apostle), the world's first animated feature. It precedes the American Winsor McCay's *The Sinking of the Lusitania* and contains 58,000 images made in 12 months while the latter has 25,000 images made in 22 months. *El apóstol*, a satire of the Radical President, Hipólito Yrigoyen, is marked by its use of popular expressions and its depiction of Buenos Aires, the river, and the port.

Alcides Greca, an anthropologist, films the feature-length *El último malón* (The Last Indian Uprising), based on the uprising of the Mocovi Indians in Santa Fé province in 1904. The first part of the film documents the impoverished living conditions of the Indians at the time the film was made. The second part recreates the event using the Indians as actors and contains a remarkable sequence where the heroine, tied to a tree, sets herself free and dashes off to save the hero from death.

1919 *Juan sin ropa* (Juan Without Clothes) is produced by Camila and Héctor Quiroga and directed by French technician Georges Benoît. The film is a dramatization of the year's "Tragic Week," the brutal culmination of years of repression against popular workers' anarcho-syndicalist unions. Pío Quadro films the documentary *La semana tragica* on the same subject.

Horacio Quiroga inaugurates the country's specialized film criticism with a column in the magazine *Caras y Caretas* (Faces and Masks.)

1920   U.S. film companies set up direct distribution subsidiaries in Argentina, and throughout Latin America, no longer allowing national distributors to handle the lucrative U.S. films. The U.S. penetration of the Argentine market has begun: for the next 10 years, until the advent of sound, Argentine films will account for only 10% of domestic box-office receipts, domestic production will decline, foreign markets will gradually be lost, and Argentina will become the world's second largest importer of U.S. films (after Australia and before Brazil).

Federico Valle begins the newsreel service *Film Revista Valle*. Valle was an Italian immigrant who studied under Georges Méliès and co-filmed, with Wilbur Wright, the first aerial photography in Europe. *Film Revista Valle* came out every Thursday at 5 p.m. for 10 years, with special editions being produced when needed, and opened up location shooting in the interior of the country. In 1926 Valle, who was uninsured, lost most of his equipment and archives in a fire. In 1930 he dissolved the company to start a classroom educational program with film that was quashed by Argentina's first military government, which deposed the increasingly left-leaning Yrigoyen that year. Valle later tried to sell his remaining archives — he had by then made over 1,000 films — but couldn't interest a film museum and sold them to a comb manufacturer for their celluloid content. Valle's work went without proper recognition until 1958 when he was given a position in the newly created *Instituto Nacional de Cinematografía* and was voted a pension by Congress a year later.

1921   100 feature films have been made in the six years since

Amalia, the country's first, was produced. At this stage of the film industry's development, only the best and most successful Argentine films actually recoup their investment, and the industry is hampered by its lack of stability and by insufficient capital investment.

The development of strong national themes in film to this date has been due in part to a close collaboration between film directors and popular Argentine novelists of the day, such as Belisario Roldán, García Velloso (himself the director of *Amalia*), and Martínez Zuviría. As the decade progresses, this collaboration, and the quality of Argentine literature itself, declines.

1922　In *La muchacha de Arrabal* (The Girl from Arrabal or The Girl from the Slums) by Ferreyra, tango music makes its first appearance in the Argentine cinema, played by a live orchestra during the projection. Ferreyra, a painter, set designer, and lyricist, wrote the lyrics to the tangos performed.

1927　The film industry enters a period of severe crisis as the domestic market is dominated by U.S. films and production falls drastically.

Ferreyra undertakes an unsuccessful international sales tour with his films but returns convinced of the need to introduce sound technology to Argentine film production.

1931　*Muñequitas porteñas* (Port Dolls), by Ferreyra, is the
[4] *　country's first sound feature, using discs. It is another important treatment of working class *porteño* life by Ferreyra.

The Argentine tango star Carlos Gardel makes 10 short films with optical sound. Afterwards, he leaves the country and makes several features in France and the U.S. in their Spanish-language studios. In 1935, on his way back to Argentina to shoot *El caballo del pueblo*, he crashes to his death in an airplane accident.

*Annual film production

1933
[6]
The first optical sound studios in Latin America are built by the firms *Lumiton* and *Argentina Sono Film*. *Sono Film* produces the first feature using optical sound, *Tango*, by Luis Moglia Barth, a Buenos Aires-after-dark film.

Fearing the loss of its foreign markets due to the advent of sound, the U.S. begins foreign language production at its studios in Hollywood and Joinville France.

The Hispanic films employ mostly Spanish technicians and are popular in Spain but have little effect on the rising popularity of Argentine films, once again, in the Latin American market. Sound technology has allowed Argentine filmmakers to incorporate not only Argentina's unique Spanish pronunciations and idioms into their films but also the rhythms of the popular tango. Despite the rapid growth of the Argentine film industry throughout the 1930's, however, U.S. films maintain a strong presence in the Argentine market.

1937
[28]
After studying 4 months at the Eastern Kodak complex in Rochester, New York, Carlos Connio Santini and his father Alejandro (Alex) Connio found the *Alex* film laboratories, Argentina's first high quality labs.

Enrique Susini's film *La chismosa* (The Gossip) wins a Mention at the Venice Film Festival, as will *Margarita, Armanda, y su padre* (Margarita, Armanda, and her Father, by Francisco Mugica) in 1939. These are the first awards given to Latin American films by a European festival.

1939
[50]
The Argentine film industry is at the height of its golden age. Argentine films are popular at home and distributed throughout the Spanish-speaking world. Mexico's production this year: 37 films.

Argentine films owe their popularity in the domestic and Latin American markets to the wide variety of popular genres being produced, each based on themes drawn from Argentine life. These genres include (with notable examples in brackets): tangos (*La vida de Carlos Gardel* — The Life of Carlos Gardel, Alberto de Zavalía,

1939; other films with the prolific singer Hugo de Carril); the "social-folkloric" genre (*Prisioneros de la tierra* — Prisoners of the Earth, Mario Soffici, 1939); historical films and gaucho epics (*Huella*, Luis Moglia Barth, 1940); crime thrillers (*Fuera de la ley* — Outlaw, Manuel Romero, 1937); urban dramas (*Calles de Buenos Aires* — Streets of Buenos Aires, José Ferreyra, 1935); "women's" melodramas (*La que no perdonó* — She Who Didn't Forgive, Ferreyra, 1936); comedies (*La rubia del camino* — The Blonde en Route, Romero, 1938); and literary adaptations (a sound remake of *Amalia*, Luis Moglia Barth, 1936).

1942 The boom continues. There are 30 studios in operation,
[56] providing regular employment to 4,000 people. Mexico's production: 42 films.

The production company *Artistas Argentinos Asociados*, formed a year earlier by a group of young nationalists, produces *La guerra gaucha* (The Gaucho War) by Lucas Demare, seen as one of the last great classics of the golden age with a popular national theme.

Production of the "social folkloric" or social problem film goes into decline. *Cruza*, by Moglia Barth, made this year, is one of the last great examples of the genre. Among the few films to follow are *Malambo*, by Alberto de Zavalía, made later this year, and *La calle grita* (Cry From the Street), by Lucas Demare, in 1948.

In retaliation for Argentina's neutrality during the war, the United States imposes an embargo on raw film exports to the country, fearing pro-Axis propaganda film production in Argentina. No raw stock enters the country this year through legal channels; producers use up their inventories and a black market emerges, supplied by neighbouring countries.

1943 Despite raw stock rationing and equipment shortages at
[36] home, the U.S., on the advice of Nelson Rockefeller's Office of the Coordinator of Inter American Affairs

(CIAA), begins an ambitious support program to the fledgling Mexican film industry. The Mexicans are lavished with equipment, stock and technical advisers and American capital begins a program of heavy investment in the Mexican film industry. Fearing both pro-Axis film production in Argentina and the popularity and sophistication of Argentina's films, the U.S. embarks on a plan to replace Argentina with Mexico as the region's largest film producer. This year, Mexico receives 11 million metres of stock, while Argentina, with a larger film industry, is allotted only 3 million.

1944
[24]
The U.S. informs Argentina that it will again increase Mexican raw stock allocations and cut shipments to Argentina and suggests that Argentina produce its own stock. The company *Delta* is founded to re-emulsion old stock but technical skills, equipment and chemicals are lacking. A small amount of stock is prepared and is used for work prints.

The embargo and poor management of the Argentine industry take their effect and production declines dramatically. The industry is hampered by poor Latin American distribution methods, an unfair domestic distribution system that works in the favour of exhibitors and not producers, insufficient capital investment, antiquated production methods that require twice the time to shoot a film as the Mexican industry, disuse of popular Argentine film stars, and a dramatic change in the themes and styles of Argentine film popular in the 1930's.

In the midst of a collapse of Argentina's foreign and domestic film markets, Argentine producers appeal to the government for protection and become involved in a bitter dispute with national exhibitors over revenue sharing. The new Secretary of Labour and Social Welfare, Colonel Juan Domingo Perón, rules in favour of the producers and legislates a scale of percentages to be paid by the exhibitors. He also legislates exhibition quotas on national films that exceed current production. Production is thus stimulated but, since every film is virtually guaranteed exhibition, corruption and adventurism are encouraged.

700 film workers found *La Asociación Gremial de la Industria Cinematográfica Argentina* (*AGICA* — The Guild of Argentine Film Workers) and demand pay raises and better working conditions.

1945
[23]
U.S. raw stock exports around the world begin to return to normal, except to Argentina. Agfa Gevaert will begin to supply the country in 1946; until then, the industry relies on black market supplies obtained in Chile and Uruguay, which have abundant supplies. *Delta* fails in its attempt to make virgin positive stock and closes. Mexico's production: 64 films.

Hugo Fregonese co-directs *Pampa barbara* (Savage Pampa) with Lucas Demare. After shooting the musical *Donde mueren las palabras* (Where Words Die), in 1946, he emigrates to the U.S. to pursue a successful career with a major studio that had been interrupted with the outbreak of war and Fregonese's forced return to Argentina.

1946
[32]
Perón is elected President of Argentina in a landslide election victory with the massive support of the country's working class. He begins to implement his vision of a hierarchical and corporatist society with generous social welfare programs and progressive labour policies. Strong ideological pressure is placed on the film industry and on other media — the opposition newspaper *La Prensa* is closed down — at the same time as the corrupt Peronist bureaucracy extends its control as well, through the state control of film stock allocations, for example.

1947
[38]
Perón, an extreme economic nationalist, strengthens the earlier protection he granted the film industry. State financial assistance is given to producers, according to a formula that encourages cheaper productions, and exhibition quotas on national films are extended. In Buenos Aires, Argentine films must be screened one week out of eight; in the provinces, the ratio is two

weeks out of five.

The film industry, meanwhile, continues on its fatal course of stylistic and thematic Europeanization and bourgeoisification. Fully one-half of all national films are now adapted from foreign sources; even the nationalist Demare films from a foreign source this year. Argentina's "white telephone" period is by now fully established and insipid comedies, bourgeois salon dramas, lavish historical productions, and European literary adaptations dominate production, at the cost of losing the domestic working class and Latin American markets.

There is a considerable movement of film talent out of the country as black and grey lists begin to appear in the industry.

1948 The *Sindicato de la Industria Cinematográfica Argentina*
[41]   (*SICA* — The Argentine Film Workers Union) is formed and suggests an increase in film admission prices to provide funds for production. Perón is adamant that prices remain frozen, as they do until three years after his overthrow in 1955, despite the rampant inflation in the country during his rule. Film admissions are the only stable prices during this period and will be the lowest in the world by 1958. A compromise is reached and exhibitors begin to pay a surcharge on their rental rates, 40% of which will be used to stimulate production (with most of the remaining amount going to the Eva Perón Foundation, Perón's wife's private charity).

1949 Only *Argentina Sono Film*, with markets in the Carib-
[47]   bean, continues to have substantial sales abroad. Mexico has replaced Argentina as the main regional supplier of the Latin American market. In the past decade, Mexico has earned $10,000,000 U.S. in foreign sales and Argentina $80,000 U.S.

The popular tango singer and actor Hugo del Carril debuts as a film director with *Historia del 900* (The Story of the 900).

1950 The government announces the formation of a distri-
[56] bution company for Argentine films abroad that will be
jointly owned by the state and private interests, as
Mexico had done years earlier, but the project never
gets off the ground.

In response to strong import barriers in Spain against
foreign films, Argentina negotiates a bilateral policy
with Spain that puts quotas on each country's film
exports to the other. Argentina proceeds to negotiate
similar agreements with other countries, but the U.S.
refuses to participate, calling for a "free trade" approach
that would see as many U.S. films in Argentina as the
market will bear. In response, Argentina suspends all
import permit issuances to U.S. distributors and only
old U.S. films are seen in Argentina until 1952. An
all-time low of 131 foreign films are screened in Argentina this year, contributing to a 30% drop in box-office
revenue since 1949. National production swells to fill
the gap. Mexico's production this year: 125 films.

1952 After filming in Spain in 1951, Hugo del Carril returns
[35] to direct *Las aguas bajan turbias* (Troubled Waters), the
last of the great rural social problem films. Its source
is the novel *El río oscuro* (The Dark River) by Argentine
communist Alfredo Varela, who is in Perón's prisons at
the time. To obtain approval to shoot the film, del
Carril had to leave Varela's name off the credits. The
film also eliminates the communist characters from the
story that were found in the novel.

1954 Veteran directors (such as Soffici and del Carril) and
[45] new directors associated with the emerging *nuevo cine*
movement (Fernando Ayala, Leopoldo Torre Nilsson)
begin to return to Argentine novelists for their sources.
In the coming years, the writers David Viñas, Juan José
Manauta, Beatriz Guido (Torre Nilsson's wife) and
Julio Cortázar become regular collaborators.

1955 The first colour feature is made in Argentina, *Lo que*
[43] *pasó a Reynoso* (What Happened at Reynoso), by vet-

eran director Leopoldo Torres Ríos, Torre Nilsson's father.

1956 One year after Perón's overthrow in a military coup,
[36] Fernando Birri returns to Argentina after studying with the Italian neo-realists at the *Centro Sperimentale* in Rome. Soon afterwards, he establishes *La Escuela Documental de Santa Fé*, a documentary film school. Birri's first film *Tire dié* (Throw Me a Dime), in 1958, about young children begging for money, is seen as the first Latin American social documentary.

Lucas Demare films *Después del silencio* (After the Silence), a film with an anti-Peronist theme that stars two formerly exiled actors, Arturo García Buhr and María Rosa Gallo. The military government in place since 1955, meanwhile, is beginning to produce its own exiles.

1957 The military government suspends all Peronist film
[15] legislation and a few months later brings in its own. A 10% tax on film admissions will finance state production subsidies. Short films, the medium of many of the *nuevo cine* directors, are particularly encouraged, and 250 will be made by 1963, though few of these will be seen commercially. The *Instituto Nacional de Cinematografía (INC)* is formed, which will suffer instability and change Directors 10 times in the coming decade. The first formal process of film censorship is established. The Peronist system of classifying films "A" or "B" is maintained: "A" status guarantees exhibition by law by virtue of the films' special interest. Exhibitors resolve not to obey this law and occupy *INC's* offices in protest. Quotas on foreign film imports are lifted, leading to the release of 697 foreign films this year, from the low of 131 in 1950.

1959 The government introduces a new economic plan and
[22] allows the peso to float. Film production costs rise 60%, with a 300% rise in the cost of chemicals, 40% in equipment, and 100% in raw stock.

Import quotas are re-imposed on foreign films. A maximum of 200 U.S. films may be imported annually along with 25 to 35 French, British, Italian, and Mexican.

The *Festival Cinematográfico Internacional de la República Argentina* is begun at the resort town of Mar del Plata. It continues annually until 1966 and bi-annually thereafter until 1970.

There is a strong drive to "internationalize" the Argentine film industry through the aggressive pursuit of prestigious foreign co-productions. Andrzej Monk is to shoot a film about the recent kidnapping of former Nazi Adolf Eichmann from Buenos Aires to stand trial in Israel, and Abel Gance plans a film on the life of General San Martín. Neither film is made.

1962 Exhibition quotas are re-imposed on national films. One
[32] Argentine film must be screened for every six foreign films. National films nonetheless account for only 8% of box-office revenues.

1963 Censorship worsens under a new military government
[27] and affects both prestigious foreign films (by directors such as Ingmar Bergman and Pier Paolo Pasolini) and national productions (by such emerging talents from the *nuevo cine* movement as Manuel Antín and Fernando Ayala). For the next decade, the censorship board will be headed by the religious and moral extremist Ramiro de la Fuente.

Fernando Birri, after making *Los inundados* (The Flood Victims, 1961) and *Pampa gringa* (1963), is forced to leave the country for political reasons. He works briefly in Rio de Janeiro and is forced to return to Italy because of a coup in Brazil in 1964.

Key members of the *nuevo cine* generation are still working in the margins of the film industry. The movement as a whole has yet to stimulate production — as in fact it never will — nor has it recaptured the lost audience for Argentine films, owing perhaps to its adherents' very European and intellectual style and introspective themes.

1968   Anticipating the widespread social unrest that will
[39]   erupt in 1969 and bring about the military government's
        downfall in 1973, Fernando Solanas and Octavio Getino
        complete *La hora de los hornos* (The Hour of the
        Furnaces). The film is circulated clandestinely through-
        out Argentina via trade unions and political organizations
        and is hailed abroad as a milestone of the emerging
        "New Latin American Cinema" movement. One year
        later, Solanas and Getino publish the manifesto "Toward
        a Third Cinema", which calls for the creation of a
        politically engaged cinema to be used in the struggle
        for national liberation.

1971   The industry experiences a shortage of raw film stock,
[36]   a recurring problem in the coming decade, brought on
        by import restrictions due to a balance of trade deficit.
        The government also imposes a 300% increase on import
        duties that affects film prints, causing the American
        Majors to temporarily withhold their films in protest.
        Massive devaluations of the peso begin — its value is
        cut in half in the final months of the year alone —
        slashing the dollar profits of foreign film suppliers
        and boosting the price of film stock and equipment to
        national producers.
            The beginnings of an Argentine *avant garde* are
        seen. Edgardo Cozarinsky films ... (*Puntos suspendidos*
        — Dot Dot Dot). The film is censored and he soon
        relocates to Paris.

1973   Before handing power over to the victorious Peronists,
[39]   who were allowed to contest an election for the first
        time in 20 years, the outgoing government of General
        Alejandro Lanusse decrees that all foreign films must be
        dubbed into Spanish in Argentina. There is some doubt
        that Argentine labs have the capacity for this much
        work, and the American Majors, fearing the effects of
        the legislation on their foreign markets (if other coun-
        tries followed suit, it would force them to dub each film

more than once in foreign labs) again withhold their films in protest.

Under Perón, a profound restructuring of the film industry begins. Hugo del Carril is named director of *INC*, Octavio Getino heads the film censorship board, and Fernando Solanas represents a new association of independent producers.

The brief period of Perón's reign is marked by: an increase in production (54 films are made during his 14 months in power, against a 30 year average of 30 films per year); the success of Argentine films in the domestic market and a huge increase in film attendance (40% in 1974); the elimination of censorship and the reform of the censorship board, which allows all previously banned films to be seen; the reform of the industry's trade unions; the encouragement of small- and medium-sized producers to stimulate and diversify production; and a return to popular national themes.

1974 The most successful film of the year is *La Patagonia*
[40] *rebelde* (Rebellion in Patagonia), by Héctor Olivera, co-owner of Aries Films with Fernando Ayala, one of the country's largest production companies. The film, which recounts a bloody confrontation between anarcho-syndicalist workers and a brutal military in Patagonia in the 1920's, produces a violent reaction from the military of 1974. Released days before the death of Perón, the film begins its wildly successful run amidst the political turmoil, bellicose statements from the military, the resumption of right- and left-wing terrorist activity, and speculation that it will be censored. Finally, it is voluntarily pulled from distribution by Aries on the grounds that it was being used as propaganda by left-wing guerrillas.

Days after the death of Perón, a sweeping new cinema bill is passed in Congress and signed by Isabel Perón, but it is never implemented. Among other things, it contains a contentious clause calling for the re-imposition of a "six to one" quota that would require one Argentine film be exhibited for every six foreign films.

After the aged Perón's death and his second wife Isabel's assumption of power, del Carril and Getino resign their positions. Del Carril is replaced by another veteran director, Mario Soffici. As an indication of the political tendencies of the Isabel Perón government, Getino is replaced by the moral and religious fanatic Miguel Tato. By the time of the military coup of 1976, Tato will have banned 160 films, by all indications a world record.

1975
[31] As the political crisis worsens and the economy is in ruins, the film industry becomes paralysed. There is widespread labour unrest in the industry as even 100% wage increases can't keep up with inflation. Very few people are working in the industry in any event: inflation; a shortage of raw stock; and the severe and erratic censorship actually bring the industry to a standstill for several weeks in mid-winter.

The first movement of film talent out of the country begins. Some people leave for economic reasons and accept job offers abroad. Others, like Sergio Renán, whose film *La tregua* (The Truce, 1973) was nominated for an Oscar, leave because of death threats from the far Right.

1976
[16] The military overthrows Isabel Perón in a coup and intensifies the terror against artists, journalists, students, teachers and trade union activists begun under her regime. The filmmakers Jorge Cedrón, Octavio Getino, Rodolfo Kuhn, Lautaro Murúa, Fernando Solanas and Gerardo Vallejo, as well as a score of actors and technicians, flee the country. Others, including Raymundo Gleyzer, of the film collective *Cine Grupo de la Base* (*Los traidores* — The Traitors, 1972) are abducted and "disappear".

The censor Miguel Tato is the only important Peronist official left in place after the coup. He bans Leopoldo Torre Nilsson's last film, *Piedra libre* (Home Free). Torre Nilsson, travelling in Spain when the decision is handed down, declares he will not return to Argentina and dies two years later.

1977 U.S. films dominate the box-office: the top 10 films this
[15]   year are all American. In 1974, 6 were Argentine. In the
       coming year, U.S. film profits in Argentina will increase
       60%.
       Argentina Sono Film, founded in 1933, closes its
       studios. *Aries* controls the country's only studios.

1979 Production is stimulated but is mainly limited to escapism
[31]   and vulgar comedies. Films like *La guerra de los sostenes*
       (The Brassiere War) and *Los hombres piensen solamente*
       en eso (Men Only Think of That) are typical of produc-
       tion under the dictatorship, and very few new filmmakers
       enter the industry.

1980 Jorge Cedrón, director of *Operación masacre* (Operation
[28]   Massacre, 1972), about the slaughter of militant Peron-
       ists in 1956 after the overthrow of Perón, dies violently
       in exile in Paris. The police consider his death a suicide
       but friends insist that he was assassinated by agents of
       the Junta. This same year, Octavio Getino is indicted
       for his activities as head of the film censor board and
       the Junta tries unsuccessfully to obtain his extradition
       from Perú.

1982 Film attendance, already a fraction of 1973-74 levels,
       falls dramatically as news of the war in the Malvinas and
       the World Cup soccer championship dominates the news
       media and national life.
           Latin America's foremost ethnographic filmmaker,
       the Argentine Jorge Prelorán (*Hermógenes Cayo*, 1969,
       Cochengo miranda, 1978) shoots his first dramatic
       feature film in Ecuador, *Mi tia Nora* (My Aunt Nora) and
       resettles in the U.S.
           The film milieu begins to organize in anticipaton of
       political change in the wake of the Junta's military
       defeat by Britain. The film magazine *Cine Libre* is
       founded and edited by filmmaker Mario Sábato. The
       first issue contains articles on exiled Chilean director

Raúl Ruiz, new Spanish cinema, and on the Argentine filmmakers Alejandro Doria, Adolfo Aristarain, and Héctor Babenco (who lives and works in Brazil). The second issue contains interviews with Fernando Birri and Lucas Demare and inaugurates a country-by-country survey of Latin American cinema with articles on Nicaragua and Venezuela.

1983 Before elections are held *SICA*, the film workers' union,
[13] organizes a "March for Argentine Cinema" in downtown Buenos Aires. The film workers carry placards demanding the return of their "missing" co-workers, and a set of demands is published, which includes an end to censorship and blacklists and a call for government stimulation of the industry.

Films begin to treat the country's political and social reality in a more open way. Héctor Olivera films *No habrá más penas ni olvido* (Funny Dirty Little War), a black comedy (from the novel by Osvaldo Soriano) on the origins of the years of terror, the blame for which Olivera lays squarely at the feet of the Peronists. The French newspaper *Le Monde* cites the film and the novel as decisive factors in the Peronists' first ever electoral loss later this year.

1984 Sweeping changes are made at the *Instituto Nacional de*
[22] *Cinematografía* following the election of Raúl Alfonsín's *Union Civica Radical (UCR)* party. The filmmaker Manuel Antín is named Director of the Institute and promises to restore production to 30 films per year. He invites filmmakers of all political persuasions to apply for state co-production assistance, which returns a 10% cinema admissions tax directly to *INC* to cover its operating budget and finance co-productions.

Congress abolishes censorship. The film critic Jorge Miguel Couselo is appointed head of the film classification board.

1985 Production levels are not as high as anticipated because
[26]+ of an early depletion of the Film Aid Fund money.

Production is halted briefly when *SICA* demands a 40% wage increase for its members, which is impossible to grant under the terms of Alfonsín's "Austral Plan", an economic program that introduces wage and price controls. The program brings Argentine inflation down to about 40% a year but a tighter rein is kept on wage increases. It also endeavours to pay Argentina's US$55 billion foreign debt, the result of the Junta's military expenditures and fiscal lunacy, on better terms than those demanded by the International Monetary Fund.

The film industry has not yet met the success of the 1973-75 period. Only 4 of the top 10 (and 5 of the top 15) films this year are Argentine. In 1974, 6 of the top 10 and 9 of the top 15 films were Argentine. Attendance in working class neighbourhoods, after rising with the return of democracy, falls because of the economic situation and the lack of Argentine films with popular themes.

Alfonsín's resolve to resist censorship is tested with the world-wide scandal of Jean-Luc Godard's *Je vous salue, Marie* (Hail Mary). The film is banned in Brazil, which has also just returned to democracy. Brazil's President succumbs to intense Catholic pressure and bans the film against the wishes of the film censor board. Similar pressure is placed on Alfonsín, and despite one powerful Catholic's claim that Alfonsín assured him that he was personally dedicated to banning the film, no such prohibition follows. However, the film is not bought by any Argentine distributor and it is not seen in Argentina.

Norma Aleandro, who acted in *Operación masacre* (Operation Massacre, Jorge Cedrón, 1972) and fled the country in 1976, stars in *La historia oficial* (The Official Story), by Luis Puenzo. Her performance earns her a shared Best Actress award at the Cannes Film Festival this year before the film wins an Oscar for the Best Foreign Film in 1986.

Fernando Solanas returns to Argentina to complete *Tangos: el exilio de Gardel* (Tangos: The Exile of

Gardel), begun in exile in France several years earlier. The film wins a Special Jury Prize at the Venice Film Festival this year. Solanas, who, with Octavio Getino, coined the term "third cinema", has invented a new term to describe *Tangos*: a *tanguedia* — part comedy, part tragedy, part tango musical. Solanas, who has a professional background in music, wrote the tango lyrics (like Ferreyra in *La muchacha de Arrabal* 60 years before him); the music was composed by the prominent Argentine tango artist Astor Piazzola. The box-office hit of 1986 in Argentina, it is for Solanas an attempt to shake his image as an *agit* filmmaker and return to a tradition of popular cinema, synthesizing elements of Argentine popular culture (the tango) with social criticism in a mainstream entertainment film.

Contributors

Tim Barnard is a film promoter living in Toronto. He has organized a retrospective of Argentine cinema for the Ontario Film Institute to accompany this publication and tour Canada. He is the author of the three-part radio feature *International Film Censorship*, broadcast on CBC Radio's *Ideas* program in 1985.

Fernando Birri is an expatriate Argentine filmmaker and theorist. From studies at the *Centro Sperimentale* in Rome in the 1950s, he founded *La Escuela Documental de Santa Fé*, a documentary film school in the Litoral region of Argentina. His films of this period include *Tire dié* (Throw Me a Dime, 1958) and *Los inundados* (The Flood Victims, 1961). In 1964 he was forced to leave Argentina and eventually resettled in Rome, where he has made the films *ORG* (1979) and *Mi hijo el Che* (My Son Che, 1985). He is currently teaching at the national film school in Cuba.

Jorge Luis Borges (1899-1986) was Argentina's most acclaimed thinker in this century. A poet and author of complex — "labyrinthine" — short stories, he developed a unique literary style with his essays, intricate webs of fact and fancy. Despite his fame and esteem, he was denied his coveted Nobel Prize ("Refusing me the Nobel Prize," he once lamented, "has become a minor Swedish industry"). His many books available in English translation include *Other Inquisitions, Fictions,* and *A Universal History of Infamy*. He died in Geneva in 1986, where he had recently resettled ("The Buenos Aires I knew no longer exists," he was quoted as saying), and where he had spent much of his childhood.

Julio Cortázar (1914-1984) was Argentina's most accomplished novelist in this century and is regarded, with Jorge Luis Borges, Pablo Neruda, Gabriel García Marquez, and Carlos Fuentes, as one of the greatest modern Latin American authors. Born in Brussels of Argentine parents, he was raised in Argentina but relocated to Paris in 1952, where he remained until his death. Some of his work available in English translation includes *The Winners, Blow-Up and Other Stories, We Love Glenda So Much,* and *A Manual for Manuel.* In addition to writing novels and short stories he wrote poetry and was a translator and amateur jazz musician.

Edgardo Cozarinsky is an expatriate Argentine filmmaker and critic who has lived in Paris since 1974. He is the author of essays on Henry James, a novel *Urban Voodoo,* and the book *Borges en/y/sobre cine,* forthcoming in an English translation. His filmmaking career began in 1971 with the experimental feature . . . (*Puntos suspendidos* - Dot Dot Dot). In France, he has made the films *Les apprentis sorciers* (The Sorcerer's Apprentices, 1977), *La guerre d'un seul homme* (One Man's War, 1982), and *Jean Cocteau: autoportrait d'un inconnu* (Jean Cocteau: Self-Portrait of an Unknown Man, 1985).

Octavio Getino is an expatriate Argentine filmmaker and critic of Spanish birth. After the 1976 Argentine coup he spent six years in exile in Peru and now lives in Mexico. In Peru, he made films and videos for the Catholic University, organized the publication of a communications journal, taught film at the University of Lima, and worked for three years in a remote rural area organizing a Communications Centre. In Mexico he has worked as a consultant on communications policy to international organizations such as UNESCO, organized a series of film publications for *UNAM* (*Universidad Nacional Autonoma de México*), continued making films and videos, and published several books, including *Notas sobre cine argentino y latinamericano* (Notes on Argentine and Latin American Film, 1984) and *Cultura, comunicación y desarrollo en américa latina* (Culture, Communication, and Development in Latin America, 1985). His films include *El familiar* (The Relative, 1973) and, as co-director with Fernando Solanas, *La hora de los hornos* (The Hour of the Furnaces, 1966-68).

He also co-founded the radical Argentine film collective *Cine Liberación* with Solanas in the 1960s and co-authored the group's influential theoretical works, including the manifesto "Toward a Third Cinema" (1969). He is presently preparing a feature film, an Argentine-Peruvian-Mexican co-production.

Alfonso Gumucio Dagron is a Bolivian filmmaker, critic, journalist, poet, and media activist now living in Bolivia after many years of exile. After studying at *IDHEC* (*l'Institute des hautes études cinématographiques*) in Paris in the 1970s, he returned to Bolivia to begin work with *CIMCA* (*Centro de Integración de Medios de Comunicación Alternativa* — Centre for Alternative Communication Media), which produces short films about the daily concerns of Bolivian workers and peasants with their collaboration in the filmmaking process. He was exiled from Bolivia following the military coup of 1980 and worked briefly in Nicaragua before settling in Mexico. He is the author of several volumes of film history, poetry, and essays, including *Historia del cine boliviano* (The History of Bolivian Cinema, 1982), *El cine de los trabajadores* (Workers' Cinema, Nicaragua, 1981) and *La Máscara del gorilla* (The Mask of the Gorilla, Mexico 1982). His films include *Señores Generales, Señores Coroneles* (Bolivia, 1976), *Cooperativo Sandino* (Nicaragua, 1981) and *La voz del minero* (The Voice of the Miner, Bolivia, 1983).

Bibliography

Birri, Fernando, *La escuela documental de Santa Fé*, Universidad Nacional de Litoral, Santa Fé, 1964.

Burns, E. Bradford, "National Identity in Argentine Films," in *Americas*, vol. 27, no. 11-12, OAS, Washington, 1975.

Burton, Julianne, *Cinema and Social Change: Conversations with Latin American Filmmakers*, University of Texas Press, Austin, 1986.

- *The New Latin American Cinema: An Annotated Bibliography 1960-1980*, Smyrna Press, New York, 1983.

Cantor Magnani, José, and Muraro, Heriberto, "La influenza trasnacional en el cine argentino," in *Comunicación y cultura* no. 5, Mexico, 1978.

Cavalcanti, Pedro C.U., "The Left in the Mallands," in *Telos* no. 53, St. Louis, 1982.

Chanan, Michael, ed., *Chilean Cinema*, British Film Institute, London, 1976.

Ciria, Alberto, *Política y cultura popular: la argentina peronista 1946-55*, Ediciones de la Flor, Buenos Aires, 1983.

Colombres, Adolfo, ed., *Cine, antropología, y colonialismo*, Ediciones del Sol - Clasco, Buenos Aires, 1985.

Corradi, Juan E., "The Modes of Destruction: Terror in Argentina" in *Telos*, no. 54, St. Louis, 1982-3.

Couselo, Jorge Miguel, *El negro Ferreyra: un cine por instinto*, Buenos Aires, 1969.

- ed., *Historia del cine argentino*, Centro Editor de América Latina, Buenos Aires, 1984.

Cozarinsky, Edgardo, *Borges y el cine*, Editorial Sur, Buenos Aires, 1974.

- *Borges in/and/on Film*, Lumen, N.Y., 1986.

Dabat, Alejandro and Lorenzano, Luis, *Argentina: The Malvinas and the end of Military Rule,* Verso, London, 1984.

de Usabel, Gaizka S., *The High Noon of American Films in Latin America,* UMI Research Press, Ann Arbor, 1982.

di Núbila, Domingo, *Historia del cine argentino,* Edición Cruz de Malta, Buenos Aires, 1960.

- *Variety* News Reports, New York 1970-1986.

España, Claudio, *Medio siglo de cine/ Argentina Sono Film,* Editorial Abril S.A./Heraldo de Cine, Buenos Aires, 1984.

Filippelli, Rafael, "Contra la realpolitik en el arte," in *Punto de Vista,* vol. 9 no. 26, Buenos Aires, April 1986.

Ford, Aníbal; Rivera, Jorge, and Romano, Eduardo, eds., *Medios de comunicación y cultura popular,* Editorial Legasa, Buenos Aires, 1985.

Getino, Octavio, *Cine y dependencia,* author's mimeograph, Lima, 1978 (reprinted in French in Hennebelle and Gumucio Dagron, eds., *Les cinémas d'amérique latine,* L'Herminier, Paris, 1981).

- *Notas sobre cine argentino y latinamericano,* Edimedios, Mexico, 1984.

Gumucio Dagron, Alfonso, *Cine, censura y exilio en América Latina,* STUNAM-CIMCA-FEM, Mexico, 2nd edition, 1984.

Hernández, José, *Martín Fierro,* Editorial Sopena, Buenos Aires, 1953.

Hernández, Arregui, Juan José, ed. (pseud.), *Argentina: como matar la cultura,* editorial Revolucion, Madrid, 1981.

Honeywell, Martin and Pearce, Jenny, *Falklands/Malvinas: Whose Crisis?,* Latin American Bureau, London, 1982.

Johnson, Randal and Stam, Robert, eds., *Brazilian Cinema,* Associated University Presses, East Brunswick, N.J., 1982.

Lipp, Solomon, *Three Argentine Thinkers,* Philosophical Library, New York, 1969.

Lozano, Jaime, *El síndrome del cine nacional,* EDI-SICA, Buenos Aires, 1985.

Mahieu, José Augustín, *Breve historia del cine argentino,* Eudeba, Buenos Aires, 1966.

- *Breve historia del cine nacional,* Alzamor Editores, Buenos Aires, 1974.

Martínez, Carlos Dámazo, "Estética y cine argentino actual: una conversación con Alberto Fischerman y Rafael Filippelli," in *Espacios de Crítica y Producción*, no. 3, Buenos Aires, December 1985.

Mora, Carl J., *Mexican Cinema: Reflections of a Society, 1896-1980*, University of California Press, Berkeley, 1982.

Ocampo, Victoria, ed. "Sarmiento: approximaciones," *Sur* no. 34, Buenos Aires, 1977.

Palacio, Ernesto, *Historia de la argentina, 1515-1976*, Abeledo-Perrot, Buenos Aires, 13th edition, 1984.

Sarmiento, Domingo Faustino, *Facundo: civilización y barbarie*, Centro Editor de América Latina, Buenos Aires, 1967.

Schnitman, Jorge, *Film Industries in Latin America: Dependency and Development*, Ablex, Norwood N.J., 1984.

Solanas, Fernando and Getino, Octavio, "Toward a Third Cinema," in *Cineaste*, vol. IV, no. 3, New York, 1970-71.

Willemen, Paul, ed., *Brazil: Post-Cinema Nôvo*, Framework no. 28, London, 1985.

In addition, the film journals *Heraldo del Cine* (trade news), *Cine Libre* (1982-1984), *Argentina Cine* (1985-) and *Cine en la Cultura Argentina y Latinamericana* (1985-) were consulted.

A number of other Argentine journals deal with cinema regularly, including *Crisis, Punto de Vista, Espacios de Crítica y Producción*, etc.

Index of Film Titles

tetto, Il, 67
Tire dié, 50, 68, 69, 70, 71,
  78 illus., 80, 86, 155, 165
To Die in Madrid, 88
traidores, Los, 94, 159
tregua, La, 93, 159
tres A son las tres armas, Las, 97
tres berretines, Los, 25
tres caballeros, Los, 37
Tres tristes tigres, 96
Tres veces Ana, 88

Ufa con el sexo, 91

último malón, El, 17 illus., 20,
  146
Underworld, 116, 118, 124

vacas sagradas, Las, 97
Valparaiso mi amor, 96
V enfrenta Blitzkrieg, 35
vereda de enfrente, La, 113
vida de Carlos Gardel, La, 149
Viramundo, 74
Viridiana, 88

Ya es tiempo de violencia, 90

Index of Individual Names

Aleandro, Norma, 162
Alfonsín, Raúl, 57, 58n, 84, 161,
  162
Alvarez, Carlos, 88
Alventosa, Ricardo, 88
Andrade, Rudá, 73
Antín, Manuel, 51, 156, 161
Antonioni, Michelangelo, 86, 96,
  109
Aramburu, Pedro, 67, 114
Arancibia, Ernesto, 85
Argumedo, Alcira, 93
Arias, Pepe, 134
Aristain, Adolfo, 161
Arnold, Matthew, 133
Ayala, Fernando, 52, 52 illus., 85,
  154, 156, 158

Babenco, Héctor, 161
Bancroft, George, 134
Bardem, Antonio, 143
Barnard, Tim, 165
Barreto, Vignoly, 85
Bejo, Miguel, 94
Bemberg, María Luisa, 59, 60
Benedetti, Mario, 93

Benoît, Georges, 20, 146
Bergman, Ingmar, 86, 88, 156
Bertolucci, Bernardo, 93
Birri, Fernando, 49, 50, 86, 87, 91,
  143, 155, 156, 161, 165, 168
Bo, Armando, 87
Bonacina, Diego, 73, 96
Booz, Mateo, 87
Borges, Jorge Luis, 115-126, 165,
  166, 168
Buñuel, Luis, 88
Burch, Noël, 96
Burns, E. Bradford, 168
Burton, Julianne, 50, 168

Cahen Salaberry, Enrique, 85
Cairo, Humberto, 18, 22, 146
Calinki, Julian, 97
Calistro, Mariano, 7n
Cantor Magnani, José, 168
Caparrós, Antonio, 93
Capovilla, Maurice, 73, 74
Capra, Frank, 31
Carpio, Jorge, 93
Carriego, Evaristo, 120, 122
Carrière, Jean-Paul, 114